OFF THE BALL

OFF THE BALL

The Football World Cup

Edited by Alan Tomlinson
and Garry Whannel

Pluto  Press

London   Sydney   Dover New Hampshire

First published in 1986 by Pluto Press Limited,
The Works, 105a Torriano Avenue, London NW5 3RX
and Pluto Press Australia Limited, PO Box 199, Leichhardt,
New South Wales 2040, Australia. Also Pluto Press,
51 Washington Street, Dover, New Hampshire 03820 USA

7   6   5   4   3   2   1

90   89   88   87   86

Set by Rapidset and Design Limited, London WC1
Printed in Great Britain by Cox & Wyman Limited,
Reading, Berkshire.

British Library Cataloguing in Publication Data

Off the ball: the 1986 football World Cup
   1. World Cup (*Football championship: 1986:
   Mexico*)
   i. Tomlinson, Alan   ii. Whannel, Garry
   796.334'66   Gv943.5 1986

ISBN 0 7453 0122 3

CONTENTS

OFF THE BALL

INTRODUCTION

Five thousand members of the world's media will soon be off to Mexico City to cover the finals of the World Cup in May and June 1986. Many of their foreign correspondent colleagues made an unscheduled trip there in August 1985, after at least six thousand people had lost their lives in Mexico's earthquake disaster.

Harry H. Cavan, senior vice president of the International Football Federation (FIFA), was quoted as saying that the 1986 Finals were now at risk: postponement was on the cards, he indicated. The internal mechanisms of the FIFA machine soon overruled Harry. Although 80 out of the 280 hotels earmarked for World Cup visitors were reported as being destroyed, and the main communications building, as well as twenty important telephone exchanges, were damaged (*Guardian* 23 October 1985), there were no problems; a few administrative hiccups perhaps, but no real problems – the stadia after all were still intact. FIFA chose simply to paper over the cracks. At least, that was now the public line.

The World Cup alternates evenly with the other global sporting spectacle, the Olympic Games. World Cup venues now switch between Latin America and Europe. There are bigger problems in finding adequately resourced host nations in Latin America than in Europe. Columbia was the initial choice to host the 1986 World Cup, but economic problems forced a switch to Mexico, itself no model of economic stability.

'Concern is also being expressed within the Mexican government about the morality of staging a sports extravaganza in the wake of a crippling disaster and at a time when the country is lurching towards bankruptcy at an alarming rate,' wrote Ken Jones in the *Sunday Mirror* (20 October 1985). That it should take a disaster of this magnitude to highlight this moral dilemma shows only too clearly how effectively the international sports spectacle helps in masking social inequalities both within and between nations. It is no secret that countries hosting global sporting spectacles have adopted the most blatant cosmetic measures to present an image of internal harmony to the world. And success at world level – Uruguay's massive football achievements for instance, in comparison with many much larger nations such as the USSR – has been seen as a means of expressing and nurturing a sense of national self-confidence.

Any understanding of the significance of the World Cup and of the forms of nationalism expressed in and through it must recognize the complexities and tensions within the development of different national identities. Nationalist sentiments are not always the same thing as the longing for national identity. The expression of national identity – say through a romantic ideal of the way Brazilian or Scottish football should be played – is a very different phenomenon from the appropriation of the Union Jack as a symbol of the extreme right, which has been one of the features of England's home and away support in recent years.

The growth of modern sport has been synonymous with the rise of the modern nation-state. At various times the 'national' element in sport has expressed a vibrant popular feeling, an assertion of collective identity. At other moments, as popular feelings become directed along populist lines, the 'national' element can be given the form of a regressive reactionary nationalism. In various ways, the pieces in this book explore the relationships between football, tradition, cultures and national identity.

In addition to the names mentioned at the end of chapters we would also like to thank Iain Chambers, and Geoffrey Nowell-Smith.

1. WHITE RIOTS: THE ENGLISH FOOTBALL FAN ABROAD

John Williams

> The sugar-coated pill is getting better still
> You think your country needs you but you know it never
> will
> *Elvis Costello*

It is confidently asserted these days that when the national side is struggling for points in order to qualify for the final stages of major international football competitions, senior English football officials lock themselves away in darkened rooms for a few moments of silent prayer. They ask not for goals or glory, as one might imagine, but rather for defeat and elimination. FA officials informed a curious press in 1984 that they were exceedingly *glad* that England failed to qualify for the final stages of the European Championships of that year, a competition won so conclusively by the French. There have been nervous tremors from the English football establishment over the Mexico World Cup, too. Further signs of a defeatist national malaise? A realist's recognition of our Third Division international football status, perhaps. Far from it.

It is not that the promise of qualification fills the eyes of the game's Good and Great with visions of a guileless (Hoddle-less?) national side struggling for parity against vastly superior combinations in weather better suited to siesta than to soccer. What runs through their minds instead, is a grim checklist of locations and dates which charts the violent and destructive passage of the English football fan abroad: Rotterdam '74 and

'83; Paris '75 and '84; Luxembourg '77 and '83; Turin '80; Oslo and Basle '81; Anderlecht and Copenhagen '82; and Bruges '84. English victories all, of course, for the lads who plough their narrow, violent and patriotic furrow across continental Europe in search of good football times abroad. But for the game's administrators, the British government and English 'popular opinion' (the Scots, Welsh and Irish point, quite rightly, to their own recent good record abroad) this shameful toll is an oft-cited source of national disgrace.

It is all the more so because, despite the setbacks and humiliations of the post-war years, the English continue to feel superior to other nations. 'A complacent sense of superiority', as one British newspaper recently put it, 'rooted in the idea that, whatever our failings, we are, somehow, more civilized than they, more secure in our democratic values.' A simple complacency, or part of the 'English problem'? There is much hand-wringing and head-shaking at home that the image we like to think 'They' have of 'Us' – the stiff-upper-lipped pinstripe and bowler – is being replaced abroad by that of the painted Union Jack face and the swift (televized) kick to the 'silly foreigner's' balls. British politicians and policy makers returning from their grillings on the continent repeat, rhetorically, the angry inquiries to which they, themselves, are simply unable to respond. Just *who* are these characters so 'alien' to the English tradition; these putrid carriers of what the popular press and our continental victims like to describe as the 'English disease'? More importantly, when and where will it all end? We now know at least part of the appalling answer to the last question. In May 1985 in the Heysel Stadium in Brussels, Liverpool fans in Europe were involved in the final, fatal act of a long-running English football tragedy. Mexico, meanwhile, prepares itself for what just might be a violent and distasteful encore.

Reams of newsprint and hours of radio and television coverage have already been devoted to the Heysel story. It was a

truly international news event. For days after the scenes in
Belgium, the streets of Liverpool teemed with foreign news
journalists and their crews, each looking for the 'Liverpool
story'. Those with 'social causes' features to write for the
European glossies went off in earnest search of graffiti-
covered walls, young heroin addicts and groups of street-
dwelling punks and skinheads for pictures to embellish their
accounts of the problems of the city's 'alienated' youth. For a
few days, bemused scouse punks made a killing from these
snap-happy foreign tourists with money to burn. They omitted
to tell their benefactors, of course, that they couldn't tell a
Lacoste tee-shirt from the Spion Kop, or that they steered
clear of the local football grounds for fear of attack by the
style-conscious, mainstream estate clones – labelled shirt,
straights and trainers – on the lookout for 'divvies' (or 'foreigners') from outside the local manor.

For the world's press, however, none of this really mattered.
Mere detail. The important thing was that here, in the streets
of Liverpool and on the bloodied terraces in Brussels, was *real*
life. The real *news* story from Heysel, as it had been from the
Munich Olympics in 1972, was that sport had been caught with
his – in the case of English football, definitely *his* – escapist
trousers down. It was the *nature* rather than the scale of the
Heysel tragedy which unfurrowed the brows of hard-pressed
features editors. Around the same time as the Heysel affair,
untold thousands of people lost their lives as a cyclone hit
Bangladesh. Here was a truly awesome human tragedy, and
yet it was dwarfed in international news coverage by Liverpool's disgrace in Brussels. This discrepancy is only partly
explicable by reference to routine Western ethnocentrism and
by the *televised* horror of Brussels. Crucially, the TV pictures
from Belgium also offered their vast international audience
the compulsive fascination of the destruction of those Western
sporting mythologies which demand that reflections of the
ugly and brutish divisions of the real world are left firmly out-

side the entrance to the competitive sporting arena.

Needless to say, the English penchant for wearing signs of its disturbed urban heartlands on the national football sleeve is viewed abroad with a mixture of bewilderment and incredulity. In the United States, a social distance between 'the product' (including the audience) and 'the streets' lies at the very heart of entrepreneurial sporting success. English football officials can only stare with wide-eyed envy at the zany orderliness of US football and baseball fans. They tinker with the English product in vain attempts to reproduce in this country the American sporting dream of the trouble-free, high spending sports crowd. The traditions and roots of the English game inhibit the effective operation in this country of the American business miracle in sport. In neighbourhoods surrounding some of the major American sporting venues – the Yankee Stadium in the Bronx or the Memorial Coliseum in Los Angeles, for example – the nation's heart beats at a faster, more threatening rate. Here, as nervous, well-heeled fans carefully pick their way back to the suburbs, the 'real world' grinds on, with rates of crime and violence soaring beyond the worst nightmares of police officials in England. A public inquiry into the serious riots which followed baseball's World Series in Detroit in 1984, riots which shocked sports administrators in America, revealed, reassuringly, that they were caused, not by fans, but by 'street kids'. Little wonder, then, that, after Brussels, American sports officials, like the National Football Leage's (NFL) Jim Heffernan, were expressing their total incomprehension at 'the kind of reality that is imposed at English soccer grounds'. The recent English football experience shows only too clearly that the grim, masculine rituals of the streets, re-enacted on the terraces and in the seats, are poor box office in the international sporting marketplace.

It is not, I hasten to point out, that English football is totally without its own myth-making guardians in this respect. Far from it. The light entertainment approach to football favoured by the major British television companies, for example, has the game uneasily balanced between reminiscences of the balmy days of calmer terraces, rosettes and centre partings, and those of present-day ventures into champagne lunches, slick sponsorship deals, executive box panoramics, and, with a nod to the all-conquering Americans, pre-pubescent drum majorettes.

The frequently abusive and obscene terrace chants and songs aimed at these young female sacrifices and at other matchday targets never make it through the final TV edit, of course. And players who were once football gang material themselves now have their every action carefully laundered for armchair consumption. In tele-talk, for example, tackles are always 'uncompromising', never dirty; players 'tangle' or 'clash' but never fight. Crowd 'problems' occur only *inside* grounds and then, ludicrously, only *off* screen with players, immobile, peering into a distance beyond the viewer's reach. Football commentators jabber endlessly over those obscene and racist chants which *do* manage to penetrate, as if afraid to let their audience hear. In the 'real' world, meanwhile, outside grounds and away from the cameras, police on match days pit their muscle against the plotted-up rival forage gangs while residents in the run-down, often multi-ethnic, areas which surround many of our ancient stadia are casually abused or attacked by young Paki-bashers down for an afternoon's 'sport' on a rival manor.

English football, in this mythical world constructed for it by television, is not the flawed product of a society scored with real divisions of race, sex and class. Football fans are not rich or poor; employed or unemployed; black or white. They are, simply, *real* fans (the silent majority) or hooligans (the mindless, isolated minority). Punters or morons. Real disasters, which unavoidably reveal the macho underbelly of the English condition, provide the sternest test of the capacity of the game and its enormous supporting cast to kick life back into soccer's twitching corpse. In short, they require the collective, restitutive surgery of what the image-management industries like to describe as the actions of 'good professionals' on top of the job.

Heysel is a case in point. The usual television studio platitudes and chit-chat could hardly be expected to cope with the televised conversion of the routine, but unheard, terrace cries of 'fuckin' spics' into sudden, horrible death. But the TV experts soon rallied, valiantly, with instant social policy to tame the hooligan; with calls for the disciplined violence of national service, for example; and with unfettered admiration for the brutal Spanish riot police who had cowed the English during the World Cup finals of 1982. Plaudits followed, too, for the BBC decision to keep the cameras rolling on the empty, worthless affair on the field while some of our continental neighbours, sickened by the scenes of the dying and the dead, pulled the television plug on Europe's biggest football occasion. The BBC's reward, of course, was a massive armchair audience which grew as the tragedy unfolded.

And who could forget the performance of the Liverpool players, some of whom began by denying any knowledge of the carnage on the terraces and ended with hollow assertions to hard-nosed pressmen about the importance of forgetting the fatal preliminaries and of 'just doing your job' like – yes, like 'good professionals'. Ironically, their Italian counterparts, revered like film stars and with salaries and lifestyles to match, showed themselves to be more in touch with *their* following by leaving the changing rooms to reason with their own angry fans.

The Liverpool lads, the scallies themselves, returned home from the battle zones with their Juvé hats and predictable matter-of-fact stories of police provocation and the 'fuckin' state' of the 'crappy ground'. And fittingly for another of the great English macho shows abroad, they also showed their eventual contempt for the local police whose fault it *really* was for 'shittin' themselves' under the English assault. Liverpool club officials, meanwhile, were able to swallow the bitter pill of disgrace only with gulps of life-giving tales of National Front (not Liverpool) inspired malevolence.

And, of course, there was the British press, with its gleeful and indignant denunciation of the 'murderers'; its invented and repellent stories about Liverpool 'gunmen' and the 'leaders' of the riot; and its narcissistic and circulation-centred public fund-raising appeals. Within days, the populars were back to their own chauvinistic breast-beating features, this time on how British holiday Romeos wipe the floor with their pathetic foreign rivals. Predictable, too, was their final, inevitable, retreat from real crisis back into the candy floss world of the personality.

Finally, of course, it was the turn of the politicians. A familiar mixture of bluster and moral outrage. The Prime Minister herself, perhaps the best old pro of them all, could be seen to be out-Saatchiing even her closest advisers by arranging a War Cabinet meeting with her fellow professionals in the newspaper industry. Surely *they* would know how to isolate the 'known troublemakers'. *They* listened. Mrs Thatcher informed the assembled all-male entourage – as if they didn't already know – of the links between the violent 'enemies within': in Ulster; on the picket lines; and at English football grounds. She warned them, too, about the irresponsible weakness of her opponents' explanations (deprivation, decay) for football's clan wars. After all, hadn't those involved at Heysel firstly procured the money to travel and then drowned themselves in drink for the occasion?

Fear of new technologies, crowd pathology and the effects of junk food had all been newly championed as causes of hooliganism in the hysteria after Brussels, along with the more usual claims for factors like unemployment and urban decline. Affluence, however, was an old government favourite. In short, according to this view, England's young Calibans had *bought* their way out of their caves. Those involved were clearly under-worked and overpaid or, merrily, unemployed and overpaid. (Witness, for example, their obsessive and expensive interest in terrace style.) But, surely, this was all *too* confusing, even to Mrs Thatcher's most faithful supporters. Affluence? In Liverpool? Only days before Heysel her own Home Office ministers had also been mapping out the links between affluence and hooliganism. Prosperous Chelsea, it was pointed out with thunderous superficiality, houses a club with a wicked following. By way of contrast, clubs drawing their support from massively depressed and deprived urban areas had *few* spectator problems. 'Take, for example,' said the minister concerned, with the air of a man for whom the bell never tolls, 'take Liverpool Football Club . . .'

The grubby politics of convenience were also keenly in evidence in the dishonourable aftermath of Brussels. Wreaths for the Italian dead arrived in Belgium from many sources, but not from the disgraced English. Instead English hands moved not to the heart but unerringly, and solely, to the pocket in the shape of financial 'compensation' for the Italian dead. It was an act starkly revealing of a lack of real compassion or understanding, of a society which increasingly shows itself on the international stage to know the price of everything and the value of nothing. A few weeks after Brussels, a number of persons injured in the football fire at Bradford actually *refused* money from a public fund set up to compensate them for *their* injuries. They explained that payment was unnecessary; that they were simply thankful to be alive. Just how are we to understand *these* strange folk?

The World Cup finals are the first major test of the travelling English since the Union of European Football Associations (UEFA) decided that continental Europe had had just about enough of the none-too-gentle attentions of 'our boys'. FIFA, with one eye on the international football bank balance,

decided, after some initial hesitation, that the English were
probably worth at least one more chance. Ironically, despite
the additional fears generated by the violence and fatalities at
Heysel, Mexico is unlikely to play host during the forthcoming
finals to large numbers of English veterans from Brussels. For
one thing, and irrespective of the knee-jerk cries of 'affluence'
following the Belgian tragedy, the costs of the South American
jaunt are, of course, prohibitive. Neither is it especially easy to
jump a plane. But there are other reasons, too, why young fans
from Merseyside and other areas give the national side a rather
wide berth these days. There is no doubt that recent economic
and social policies have spiced traditional football enmities
between north and south, for example. More prosperous
southern fans increasingly taunt their northern rivals on match
days in England with gibes about unemployment and poverty.
Government policies *have* accelerated economic decline in the
north. As a result, the national football team – resolutely tied
to its southern base of Wembley – is identified by many young
fans in areas like Liverpool as representative, less of a united
nation, than of a discredited national government. Rather like
the Basques, with their disregard for the Spanish national side
and their earlier hatred for Franco's all-conquering Real Madrid, young football followers in Liverpool, a city ravaged by
the effects of recent government policies, exhibit a scathing
lack of concern for the national football enterprise, for the performance of 'Her' team.

The identification of the national side with uncaring Conservative policies will not, however, prevent *all* English fans from
attempting the journey to Mexico. Advanced warning of their
plans came immediately after Brussels. A group of southern-
based England followers accompanied the national side on the
summer tour of South America. With them they took banners
which identified them with the National Front, and one which
carried a grossly offensive slogan about those fans killed in
Belgium. Their number will almost certainly grow this summer

despite the desperate attempts of the British authorities to prevent their passage abroad. They are the advance guard of the self-styled 'Barmy Army' of England fans who have battle honours stretching around the European continent and, last summer, into Brazil and Peru. If they surface in Mexico in style, it is likely that England will be thrown out of the competition and, almost certainly, out of international football.

At the present time, the regularly violent and destructive antics of English fans leaves most of their foreign competition on the starting blocks. But there *is* action elsewhere. Many of the South American nations, for example, have a long history of spectator disorderliness. More recently, in 1985, the entire Argentinian League programme was suspended following crowd violence in the capital. Just prior to Brussels, ten spectators died after a crowd panic at a match in Mexico City itself. Countries in Western Europe, such as Holland and West Germany, carefully monitor their own domestic hooligan problems, lest they approach English proportions. A recent case in West Germany involved the 40-strong neo-Nazi 'Borrussia Front' who operate out of Dortmund and compete with rival groups in Hamburg, Munich and Frankfurt. They specialize in attacks on Turkish immigrants and engineering football match fights. Neo-fascist Spanish groups tangled with the English in Spain in 1982. Similar groups in Greece issued threats to visiting England fans later that year. Italian clubs harbour their own well-heeled and highly-organized fascist gangs in Rome, Milan and Turin. In Rome last June, slogans appeared on walls overnight congratulating Liverpool fans on their deadly performance in Belgium, though they did not mention the knife attacks on Merseysiders in the same city a year earlier. In France, at around the same time, three young men expressed their solidarity with the English by taking over the offices of the French Sports Journalists' Union in Paris and daubing the walls with ammonia, paint and human excrement. Such examples, of course, will not surprise anyone who has travelled abroad with the English and watched as small, respectful groups of foreign skins have approached their television idols from across the channel with a view to joining the all-conquering English football army.

Following the national disgrace brought by Brussels, the English press, unsurprisingly, trawled the world for hooligan tales to allay the national guilt. Admittedly, they were not difficult to find. They included: attacks on Spanish players by masked gangs; fights between rival Greek gangs at a petrol station on the national highway; reports of skinhead football rivalries in France; hooligan arrests in gentle Salzburg in Austria; violent xenophobia among the Chinese following World Cup defeat by Hong Kong; accounts of vandalism and fighting involving fans in Poland and in the Soviet Union. The list is almost endless.

There are, of course, certain satisfactions to be drawn from seeing our own football problems mimicked, for example, by the Chinese; or from noting that the Greeks have their own motorway showdowns; or that tanked-up troublemakers operate East as well as West of the Iron Curtain. (There might even be a certain amount of envy at the way a planned economy deals with drunken fans. The Soviets threaten them with loss of holiday privileges and the forfeit of places in the housing queue.) But it is a safe bet that few, if any, of these domestic dust-ups will be on public show in Mexico or elsewhere. The English, as usual, will probably perform in splendid and perfect isolation. They will take to the streets and the guest houses and not to the air-conditioned hotels and the luxury coaches. They will drink a lot. And they will fight.

Admittedly, only England has, thus far, witnessed the development of a complex national network of football gang rivalries which has helped to prime terrace regulars for the greater adventures – at football and on all-male drinking holidays – abroad. 'Abroad' here, it should be explained, is a dreamland where the bars never close, the shops are poorly-guarded, the streets and football grounds are not yet English-proof and no one ever gets nicked. This might partly explain the attraction of the continent to some of our terrace heavies. Or, is it that the English *export* their football violence abroad as a hangover from our imperial and warlike past? In these terms, Heysel and other 'triumphs' represent less a breakdown in standards and a fracturing of cultural traditions than they do a continuation and confirmation of our violent disregard towards, and our collective contempt for, those not 'To the Manor Born'. The focus that the present English national side provides for the expression of macho nationalist and racist sentiments is not just a reflection of a post-Falklands urge to nail the 'Great' back into Britain. The 'Rule Britannia' brigade also speak more deeply of our national culture and of the place of football in it.

International matches abroad ought to be an instructive source of comparison for the English. The groups of continental skinheads and leather boys, who gather, nervously menacing, at games in countries like France, Holland and West Germany look strange and incongruous in the suburban streets and park land which surround many continental stadia. They also look curiously out of place among the males *and* females and their kids, who assemble for these prestigious affairs. They *are* the much-trumpeted 'hooligan minority' we hear so much about at home. (Hence the trip by foreign journalists, not to the impoverished macho haunts of the Liverpool council estates, but to the punk and skinhead hangouts.)

Indeed, troublesome fans on the continent generally seem to conform much more closely to classic images of alienated and isolated youth than do our own streetwise terrace hard cases who merge easily into English football's murky and macho matchday fabric. The atmosphere of major international matches and of football culture abroad – certainly that of continental Europe – does feel identifiably *different* from that of the aggressive, male-dominated affairs at home. It *is* more urbane, more cosmopolitan, less, much less drunken – more *tolerant*. (This is one reason, of course, why a drive for more female fans in England needs to be supported. It is the *ideologies* which underpin the present campaign for a new, 'family audience' which require deep scrutiny.) The fans involved at the throwing and fighting end at Heysel and at England's matches on the continent may well be pronounced by their colleagues to be 'out of order', but they are hardly *out of place* abroad among the all-male drinking crews bent on getting 'off their heads', the drunken determination to do down anything which is identifiably foreign, and the obsessive, parochial concern, on and off the local patch, with 'yer own'. These trends, despite the indignant protestations of politicians, are not alien to or isolated from those more widely held in British society. They are apparent, for example, in our daily news coverage of local and foreign affairs and in the violent rantings of parliamentary spokespeople for 'revenge' on the terrace gangs. The Rambo-like xenophobia of such fans, their anti-intellectualism and racism and their Page Three sexism may be forged in mean streets and massaged by the popular rags, but such values also echo way beyond these dark passages.

The National Front, or organizations like it, will almost certainly be in tow at England's matches in Mexico, adding to our poor international image. But can the football authorities and the British Government *really* complain if they are? Racist abuse has been aimed, unchallenged, at black players in England for years. It is either ignored or casually dismissed by the game's administrators as 'just the latest fashion'. After all, they argue, mixed football gangs (black and white youths) attack Asians and their properties. How, therefore, can this be racist? Sales of football-adapted racist memorabilia and literature outside grounds on match days are, according to the clubs, simply matters for the police. When pressed on the issue, clubs produce their 'balanced' and limp statements

about wanting no political links of any kind. Anti-racist football movements are rubbished because of the threat they pose
to the game's image. Researchers and journalists are denied
access to black players if the race problem is the reason for
their interest. White players are simply 'not interested' in the
issue, or harbour their own prejudices after seasons of force
feeding in the boot room about the importance of 'hitting the
black early' because 'they' – like the prissy continental ball
players – lack bottle. Courage, stamina, heart and guts. These
are still the staple diet of the English game on the park as well
as on the terraces. According to football's engine rooms and
the terrace gangs, 'aliens', at home and abroad, lack them all.

   In the scramble for single-factor explanations for the carnage of Brussels, the National Front also figured high on many
official lists. How ironic, then, that only days before the
tragedy the British government was, once again, hauled
before the European Court of Human Rights because of its
racist immigration policies. The country which still prides itself
on 'playing by the rules' will, as it has done so frequently in the
past, simply ignore this one. How telling, too, that the present
administration's growing list of 'enemies within' includes the
pickets and the football heavies but finds no place for the per-
petrators of the escalating number of racist attacks in run-
down inner city areas. Presumably, stands of this kind are
ruled out of court because they cannot be guaranteed to produce the very special diet upon which politicians grow fat –
electoral votes. Also these examples, depressingly, don't even
begin to cover the routine *sporting* hypocrisies which make a
mockery of claims that politics and sport can or should be kept
apart. Last year, in Chile, Pinochet's troops tore down NF-
emblazoned Union Jacks during England's visit to the Chilean
national stadium. The match was played at the site where
thousands of the opponents of Pinochet's internationally-
reviled military dictatorship were tortured and murdered.
There was, of course, no discussion about the *politics* of the

English visit to Chile. Nor is it reported whether the British Government apologized to its Chilean hosts for its own fascist intruders.

So, here's to Mexico. To the bars and the brawls; to the stolen goods and the Union Jacks; to the Mexican police; and to the 'spics' and the 'wops' the world over. The watching international audience is likely to learn more about the English than they think, and so will we – more perhaps than we are willing to believe or admit.

2. TUNNEL VISION: TELEVISION'S WORLD CUP

Christine Geraghty, Philip Simpson and Garry Whannel

One November night two years ago, a visitor walking back to a university lodging room in the torrential rain, was able to hear through an open window the familiar tones of John Motson describing a match between Everton and Arsenal. Nothing unusual about this, except that the temperature was 87 degrees, and the room, full of Chinese people, was in the middle of Malaysia. Talking to them revealed not only that they knew more about English football than about the domestic Malaysian league, but also that they knew more about the current English scene than many English fans. Not only has television football become a global phenomenon, but a western-oriented view of the sport has become the norm in much of the world.

For all this, the television football which we see in Britain is still remarkably parochial. Outside of the World Cup, we rarely see any extensive coverage of matches not involving British interest. Coverage in Britain of the 1984 European Nations Cup was drastically curtailed once England failed to qualify. Indeed, the irony of television football is that while the development of broadcast technology has given us access to the international world of football, English television's way of presenting and framing the sport has done little to challenge our insularity or foster and develop the audience's understanding of football in other countries.

Television now has staggering ability to relay high quality images of live sport from around the world. From the earliest days, there has been a drive to produce immediate coverage, with ever greater realism, broadcast it over ever greater distances, and to acquire ever greater control over the images. The 1934 World Cup in Italy was covered on film, sometimes involving as many as 24 cameras at up to eight games. Newsreels were shown in cinemas within 48 hours (Roger Macdonald, *Soccer – A Pictorial History*, Collins 1977). England saw its first television football on film in 1936, and by the late 1930s Germany was pioneering live television relays of football to public viewing rooms in Berlin. The establishment of Eurovision in 1954 made it possible to extend live television across national frontiers and made the 1958 World Cup in Sweden available to much of Europe. The introduction of satellites during the 1960s meant that live pictures of Mexico in 1970 could be sent to much of the world.

Meanwhile, from 1960 onwards, advances in video recording and micro electronics began to give greater control over the television image. Action replay, slow motion and stop motion were first introduced for the 1966 World Cup in England, and colour followed in time for the 1970 contest. New lightweight cameras and sophisticated radio link-ups enabled television to penetrate behind the scenes into the players' tunnel, and even on occasion into the dressing room itself. By the 1980s, Quantel techniques further extended the ability to play with multiple images and split screens.

Football coverage on television embodies a number of conflicts and tensions. The internationalism made possible by the technology conflicts with the (English) nation-centred view of the football world offered by television. The desire of the specialist football fan has to be set against the need of television to win and hold a broader audience. The high degree of realism offered by match coverage exists in an uneasy relation with the addition of extensive replays, previews and post mortems designed to frame and explain events. Commentaries oscillate between the impartial mode used to cover club football, the unashamed commitment mode used to cover England's matches against foreign teams, and the uneasy semi-impartiality adopted when England play Scotland, Wales or Northern Ireland.

Television developed a programme format based on recorded highlights augmented with replays, analysis, discussion and interview that saw its greatest popularity with BBC's *Match of the Day* in the early 1970s. ITV's ill-fated attempt to gain exclusive football coverage eventually resulted, after intervention by the Office of Fair Trading, in an alternation of Saturday night football between BBC and ITV. The audience habit of watching Saturday night football on BBC was broken, and television football has been struggling ever since to hold on to a declining audience. This struggle has not been helped by the declining public interest in football and the rise in popularity of other television sports, such as darts and snooker, which have recently begun to get larger television audiences than football. The current professional wisdom within television is that audiences now prefer live sport, and the two channels are currently locked in a dispute with English football over how much live coverage the Football League are prepared to allow, and at what price.

The growing popularity of panels of experts in the 1970s was a response to two conflicting impulses: analysis and entertainment. A growing proportion of sports coverage of major events has become occupied by preview and post mortem discussions. This introduction of analysis might have proved a positive development, but the panels of experts that have become a permanent feature of major event coverage since the early 1970s, are a strange amalgam. They offer analysis, but there is also a strong tendency for the personalities of the contributors to become more important than their comments. Nowhere is this tendency clearer than in the recent history of ITV's *On The Ball*. Ex-international star players Ian St John and Jimmy Greaves achieved great success by a carefully judged mixture of analysis, personality and a welcome public exposure of some of the internal humour and in-jokes of the football world. But personality has emerged as the key element with the transformation of the programme, now renamed *The Saint and Greavsie*, pushing the two performers towards staleness and self-parody.

One of the consequences of the global spread of television in a form dominated by the economic power of the western countries has been that the conventions of football coverage have become international. Such was not always the case. The development of television in different countries seems originally to have involved stylistic differences. Styles do not of course remain consistent over time, but gradually modify each other. However some foreign responses to the pictures provided to the rest of the world by a BBC/ITV consortium during the 1966 World Cup reveal a variety of attitudes as to how football should be covered. The responses found much to praise in the British coverage, but also a degree of unease with a visual style more elaborate than their viewers' customary fare. German television found that 'the sudden change of cameras in critical phases of the game was very disturbing'. Mexican television reported that 'too much close-up technique was used in the games, sometimes producing a miscontinuing of the game'. NRK of Norway said that 'Since we had to do our commentary off-tube from London, we were rather hampered by the prevailing close ups or narrow pictures.' Yet the global transmission of such pictures in itself affects the way people see the game. *Le Figaro* commented, 'It will no longer be possible for us to watch a televised football match other than through the eyes of English cameras.'

The 1966 World Cup was a watershed in football coverage. For the first time in Britain, the competition received saturation coverage on television and live pictures were beamed to many other countries. Before the start of competition there was considerable public hostility to the amount of television coverage planned, but much of this hostility evaporated as an ever growing audience became gripped by England's progress towards their first and only World Cup triumph. This illustrated all too clearly that television football was capable of reaching people only marginally interested in the game and underlined a belief within television that committed football fans were only ever going to be a ·small proportion of the potential audience.

By 1970, the World Cup was well on the way to becoming a global television spectacular. Heat and high altitude were major problems for teams in Mexico, and the problems were heightened by the new economic power of television:

> Too many games were played in noonday heat merely to satisfy European television companies eager to televise games at peak viewing times. England, for example, played their vital group match against Brazil at noon, in temperatures of nearly 100 degrees and there was barely an England player who had not lost 8–10 pounds in weight.
> (Philip Evans, *World Cup 1982*, Knight 1982)

The 1970 World Cup in Mexico coincided with a British general election, and on BBC the football was given four times as much coverage as the politics. In election week alone BBC offered 31 hours of football. By contrast, the West German audience saw only 16 hours throughout the entire tournament, despite the fact that their team reached the final. Milton Shulman, (in *The Least Worst Television in The World*, Barrie and Jenkins 1973) speculated that the Labour government's plans for a quiet election masked by the football coverage were sabotaged when England were eliminated and the nation's attention returned to politics. Whether Wilson's demise can really be linked so clearly to Ramsey's must remain a matter for doubt, but the World Cup had certainly become a major national television event.

Responses to the 1966 coverage had indicated that there were stylistic variations in the coverage style of different nations, and such variations were still a feature in 1974. A detailed study of the 1974 coverage found that West German television appeared to use a more 'neutral', less mediated style – longer shots, fewer close ups – than British television (*Football on Television*, edited by E. Buscombe, BFI 1975).

However, the growing internationalization of television sport seems also to be leading to an internationalization of the conventions of coverage. During preparations for the 1978 World Cup in Argentina, representatives from the European Broadcasting Union (EBU) discovered that Argentinian football coverage used a completely different set of camera positions from that accepted in Europe:

> We didn't want to upset the hosts, but the standard of coverage was just not up to European expectations. So we took extracts from British and European coverage, held seminars for the Argentine cameramen, directors and producers, and pointed out all the faults in our own work. On this basis they accepted the system we adopt.
> (Bill Ward, head of EBU's 1978 World Cup operations group, quoted in *Broadcast* 21 November 1979)

So impressed were the Argentinians with the European conventions of football coverage that they even altered three brand new stadia to accommodate the 'correct' camera positions. The World Cup operation was used as a base for establishing Argentina's first nationwide television service, which, after EBU advice, adopted the 625 PAL colour standard. Cash gained from the sale of World Cup rights enabled them to order cameras from Bosch Fernseh, video recorders from RCA, and a range of microwave links from French, US and Japanese suppliers. Games in the 1978 World Cup were timed to coincide with peak time television in Western Europe.

This trend has continued. The whole structure of the 1982 event in Spain was designed to provide European television with a large supply of live football at the most desirable times of the day. Pye TVT have already contracted to supply £30 million worth of equipment to Mexico's Televisa for the 1986 World Cup, including 9 outside broadcast units and 100 Philips computerized cameras. Televisa plan a further escalation in the technological arms race of sport coverage; they are intending to use 10 cameras at every match. This desire to be able to show and replay events from multiple angles is apparently part of a tendency to Americanize world sport coverage, in the wake of the 1984 Olympic Games.

Because of the cost of its global infrastructure and extensive capital investment, television needs to win an audience for its coverage. It has never failed yet, but each time new problems appear. For British television, England's failure to qualify at all during the 1970s constituted a problem, only partly resolved by the dramatic presence of Scotland in 1974 and 1978. The process of building interest starts long before the final stage, as our attention is engaged with the dramas of the qualifying rounds. But only in the summer of 1986 will the World Cup briefly dominate television sport. Until then, the qualifying rounds have to compete for attention with domestic football and other sporting events. How far television can succeed in building our interest in the World Cup depends not only upon the inherent drama of football itself but also upon the conventions of television's sport coverage.

It has become commonplace to criticize television's treatment of football for its concentration on goals, goals and more goals. The weekly TV compilation programmes in England, *Match of the Day* and *The Big Match* certainly did tend to equate highlights with goals, but this is not entirely fair as a criticism. In dealing with sport generally, television is uniquely able to present the drama and emotion of a game, particularly through an emphasis on the personalities involved. In sports like tennis and snooker, the close-ups of McEnroe or Jimmy White between points give the viewer access to the emotions and pressures which are a crucial part of the pleasure of sport viewing. In sports like athletics or golf, television is able to present individuals in competition not just in the field, but in terms of their different personalities and lifestyles – Ovett and Coe, Budd and Decker, Ballesteros and Watson. Television brings to sport the values that it seeks in other forms of entertainment – an emphasis on spectacle, star individuals, and swift emotional action. Purist fans' criticisms of such an approach are unjustified, inasmuch as drama and emotion are intrinsic to watching the sport even outside the context of television. Clearly, television sport is addressing a large mixed audience within which committed fans are a minority. Nevertheless, while it is true that television can take and repackage the drama and emotion, it finds it much harder to accommodate other pleasures of sport spectating such as discussion and analysis of tactics and the skills of teamwork.

It is in this context that television's coverage of football should be seen. Football, a team game taking place in a playing area which does not neatly match the screen, does not fit television's dimensions as successfully as sports like tennis or snooker. Nonetheless, football can still be presented as an event for all viewers, not just for football fans. The FA Cup Final is such an event for English viewers, with its all-day build-up of interviews, quizzes, nostalgic clips and minidramas. Internationally, the World Cup itself is also an event for all, couched in nationalist terms – the invitation being to watch England (or Scotland or Wales) beat the rest.

The qualifying rounds of the World Cup are not, however, so focused and dramatic, and the format of this stage of the competition poses certain problems for television. It is played on a league basis, so that it lacks the dramas of instant knock out, and it takes place over a long period of time, with months between the relevant matches. On English television, it is one

of a number of attractions on offer within the sports programmes and it has to compete with a range of other sports as well as
with domestic football material. The problem, then, is that this
long-running story has no guaranteed happy ending and also
that it lacks the glamour of a one-off event.

One answer was indeed not to feature it too strongly. This
was certainly the case in the spring and early summer of 1985,
when domestic league and cup struggles offered more dramatic stories. On 22 April 1985, for example, BBC *Grandstand*'s
round-up programme *Football Focus* had a brief item on the
World Cup games to be played that week, but it was placed at
the end of the programme, after items on the English and Scottish Leagues and the European Cup. Clearly, stories like the
rise of Jim Smith's Oxford to the First Division or the return of
Everton to the top of the league fitted more neatly into television's concept of what was entertaining football coverage and
its assumptions about the insular horizons of its audience.

Nevertheless, when World Cup football is shown, the main
strategy for engaging the viewers' interest is to replace identification with particular personalities by identification with a
national team. This seems obvious, but it is a more complex
process than appears at first sight. There is very little interest
shown in 'foreign' qualifiers, even those who might be
expected to produce good football, such as Brazil or France.
But English television is able to 'adopt' other British teams –
Wales and Scotland in particular, Northern Ireland and even
by sleight of hand, Eire – in which English league players are
involved. Such a process creates some drama in tracing the different routes followed and comparing the performances. It
certainly removes the problem of concentrating on one team
and offers the possibility of a back-up if England fail either to
qualify or to produce the kind of entertainment required. *Football Focus* on 4 May 1985 was able to introduce its round up
of the week's World Cup events with Wales's three goals against
Spain rather than England's goal-less draw in Rumania.

The current England team present problems in that they do not conform to television's demands for spectacle and drama. There is an assumed inevitability that they will progress (based more on the legacy of 1966 than on the virtues of the current team) and this reduces tension. England are deemed to be Britain's senior team, but in television terms they are in a double bind, since if they qualify it is only to be expected and if they lose they are failing in professionalism. In an effort to deflect this notion of England's God-given right to be in the finals, manager Robson and coach Howe in their pre-match interviews, continually emphasize how tough and hard it is going to be. 'They're never easy games until they're won', as Howe is quoted as saying.

The lack of drama in England's progress is reinforced by this emphasis on hard work. The England team in the 1986 World Cup build-up lacks the excitement of personality and incident which television relishes. The coverage has attempted to build up English stars only to have them fade before our eyes. The enigmatic (or lazy) Hoddle might have played the role had he been picked regularly; Hateley was scarcely established in English football before he was whisked off to Italy; the captain, Bryan Robson, was affected by injury and his aggressive running faded. Emlyn Hughes's complaint during BBC's *Sportsnight* coverage of the Rumanian game at Wembley – that the English forwards did not run at defenders – voiced television's demand in a footballer's language and shows that the two worlds are not so separate. The vacuum left by this lack of glamour is filled by notions of hard work, professionalism, tireless running and solid midfield play. There is no room for excesses of emotion or skill here, only acknowledgement of a job well done. Bobby Robson's interview for the BBC after the goal-less draw in Rumania exemplified this. He said that he had done what he had come to do: 'I'm pleased. I think the nation should be.'

It is perhaps not surprising then that television's summoning-up of English nationalism is somewhat low-key. There is of course the assumption that 'we' all want England to win but there is no expectation that players will be inspired to play above themselves when playing for England. There are surprisingly few interviews with England players. Instead the emphasis is on the England manager and the pains and difficulties of his job. 'Is this the worst time for you?' begins one *Football Focus* interview, which continues by asking whether Robson is worried about it all going 'too well'! England managers from Ramsey onwards, whatever their previous persona, emerge on television as exhausted, drained and deadened. Emotion is suppressed in the interests of doing the job professionally; drama is drained away. It may be that the story with the most potential in England's build-up was not the team's progress but the fate of their manager. England's steady accumulation of points meant that this story never got off the ground. Even so, success could not erase the image. 'Not looking the life and soul of the party,' commented Barry Davies as the television showed a picture of Robson hunched on the bench at Wembley, and indeed the experience of being with England comes over on television as being a singularly difficult and joyless one.

The possibilities offered by Scotland and Wales, on the other hand, fit much more readily into television's accommodation of sport. Television is able to pick up on crowd fervour and notions of Celtic national identity. Helped by the draw which put Scotland and Wales into the same group, it is able to rework sport and nationalism in order to offer football much more convincingly as entertainment.

Firstly, neither Scotland nor Wales are expected to qualify automatically; indeed it was likely that one would only do so at the expense of the other. A clear narrative was therefore set up, centering on which team would be successful. Qualifying for these teams is not seen so much as a question of professionals doing a job well or badly: it depends far more on the passion and inspiration generated, as the cliche has it, by the players pulling on their national shirts. Every match is presented as high drama. 'An Arctic circle night red hot in importance for Scotland' was how Brian Moore introduced the Iceland v Scotland match. With the Wales v Scotland game, the long slow process of the qualifying round could be forgotten and it could be treated as a knock-out game, an event comparable to the Cup Final. The mathematics of the group were deliberately pushed to one side: 'when the temperature drops, I'll explain it'. Moore expressed the drama in strong terms: 'If anybody was expecting a classic in footballing terms tonight they were fools because it was always going to be too much red meat about this night for that to happen, but it's pulsating and nerve tingling stuff for all that.'

Secondly there is much greater emphasis on the personalities and stars in the Welsh and Scottish teams. This is true of course of the dynamic duo of Rush and Hughes, and Hughes was picked out for interview after his spectacular goal against Spain. The directness and eagerness of Hughes in particular provided an implicit contrast with England's less productive strikers. In addition, the Welsh teams contained a number of characters well known through years of performances for Wales – Joey Jones is one and Micky Thomas, picked out by Brian Moore for his terrier tactics, is another. Scotland pose rather more of a problem to the insular English in their use of 'unknown' Scottish league players but Dalglish and Souness are established stars and others like Strachan and Speedie are well known to English followers. In some ways it is the image of the Scottish team as a whole which is important to the drama – a vulnerability and carelessness when things are going well; a capacity for self-destruction which adds to the tension.

Thirdly, there is the strong emphasis on crowd identification with the teams, a fanaticism which combines football and nationalism to produce crowds that are noisily partisan. Even in Iceland, the strength of Scottish support was marked by pictures of the banners in the stadium, and after the game it was not the manager, but Scotland's best known fan who was interviewed – Rod Stewart, who remarked that he wouldn't miss the game in Wales 'for my life'. Compared with the half-empty Wembley, there can be no doubt that the noise and atmosphere generated by the Scottish and Welsh supporters was crucial to television's presentation of the game as a special event. The noise was continually present on the sound track, and was referred to by the commentators as a source of tension and pressure. At the end of the game, with Scotland manager Stein's impending death unsuspected, the cameras moved across the banks of waving Scottish banners, as if to acknowledge their contribution to the spectacle.

On English television, this Celtic drama can be watched as if by neutrals – 'we can put our feet up', as Jim Rosenthal said at Cardiff. The English presenters adopt a neutral attitude which allows nationalist positions to be firmly placed in a way that they never are in England games. In Cardiff, Brian Moore provided the balanced viewpoint between the partisan comments of Ian St John and Terry Yorath. The 'we' which is so unproblematically assumed in commentaries on England games was split here. Remarks like 'we're giving the ball away' or 'let's keep our fingers crossed' made sense to the audience only if it understood that different national positions were being expressed. Ironically, the balancing role given to Moore reinforced the ultimate chauvinism operating behind English television's use of Wales and Scotland in the World Cup build-up – the sense of English superiority which accepts with relish what they have to offer but still maintains its position of looking down on 'the bear garden'.

Another consequence of television's emphatic identification with British sides is that viewers are given little opportunity or encouragement to take an interest in teams that may be playing in qualifying rounds but not in the same groups as Eng-

land, Scotland, Northern Ireland or Wales. Results from those
groups featuring European nations are regularly reported, and
goals from these matches are shown. But, at this stage of the
competition, there is no analysis or description of historically
important World Cup sides such as France, Poland, West Germany or Yugoslavia. Past success and present form are
acknowledged: the fact that France might not 'grace' the finals
was noted by Alan Parry, and Jimmy Greaves called France
the best team in Europe. (*On The Ball*, 14 September 1985)
No comparisons are made, though; we are not encouraged to
ask why France, for example, are seen as successful and 'graceful' and England are seen as professional and struggling.

This lack of interest in non-British teams (with the exception
of Eire) is carried over even to those sides playing against England in the qualifying rounds. Because groups are seeded,
sides like Turkey, Finland and Rumania seem unlikely to
reach Mexico, but this should not automatically mean that
they are seen merely as potential sources of obstruction or
frustration. Little attempt is made to establish what a match
might mean to the opposition, especially in terms of the state
of the game in these countries, or the way the game is set up in,
for example, Rumania. When the team's names are shown
before the match, one or two players are singled out as likely to
give England trouble, but most often the only players mentioned are those who play in the leagues of a soccer 'super-
power' like Italy, West Germany, Belgium, France or England. It's as if such players had no significance within their own
national context.

When the match begins, match commentators usually make
an effort to pronounce the unfamiliar names, but the experts in
the stadium or in the studio reinforce the view that Finland or
Rumania are of less importance than England, by referring to
the opposing side only as defenders or attackers. When coverage of the match, especially from abroad, is live, the images
often suggest a different story from that told by the commen-

tators. Brian Moore could talk of England being in danger of 'putting themselves two goals down' against Finland. He didn't make much attempt to help the viewer analyse or understand how the Finnish side were handling England's supposedly more professional attacks and setting up their own. In the England v Rumania game, half-time comment concentrated on England's defence and Rumania's offside play, although nobody took up Bobby Charlton's pre-match warning that 'these Rumanians are well wound-up' and that it would be a 'physical battle'.

This failure to present the game in anything other than strongly nationalistic terms is not unique to English television. Radio Telefis Eireann (RTE) coverage of the Eire v Norway match laid greatest emphasis upon it being the decider for the Irish Republic, although the match had just the same importance for Norway. The Irish commentator, George Hamilton, drew attention to the five Norwegian players who played in other European leagues, but his after-the-match comment was exclusively about Ireland's failure and its consequence for their team.

Admittedly, it is not easy or, perhaps, possible to present a match in which a British side is involved in a completely dispassionate manner, and to do so would misrepresent the partisan nature of international competition. Furthermore, the seeding process together with the league, rather than knock-out competition of the early rounds, tends to encourage the belief that certain teams are self-evidently more important than others. But the English, or even British nationalist perspective adopted by television at this stage of the World Cup has the effect of denying that the Finnish, Rumanian or Turkish national sides might be worth a closer look in their own context rather than in relation to England. Indeed television reproduces the insular concerns of its own audiences in presenting such teams as marginal. It also ignores the possibility that France, West Germany or Yugoslavia might be offering more exciting soccer for television.

One irony of television's presentation of the World Cup is that a global communication system is harnessed towards the reassertion of national insularity. Mexico has assembled the most elaborate technological system to date for covering the game, and the television channels of the world are therefore offered extensive resources in their attempts to construct entertaining presentations. But as ever, the limitless technological opportunities are governed by the more restricted cultural horizons, amounting at times to tunnel vision.

With thanks to John Caughie, Martin McLoone and Tony Pearson for valuable material assistance.

3. NAMING THE GUILTY MEN: MANAGERS AND MEDIA

Stephen Wagg

> It scares me. All those people I don't know, sometimes
> they're so emotional. I mean, if they love you that much
> without knowing you, they can also hate you the same way.
> Marilyn Monroe

We live, perhaps more than we sometimes recognize, in an increasingly individualistic society. Most of us prefer to believe that when things happen it is because individuals – invariably famous ones – have made them happen. Whether a column of demonstrators is calling for 'Maggie, Maggie, Maggie' to be 'out, out, out', or a strike by thousands of workers is being claimed by newspapers to be the work of their leader alone, the result is the same. Although this tendency is more pronounced in some societies, notably western capitalist ones, there are few societies where, in times of consternation, the urge to hold a particular individual responsible has been resisted. Few people know this better than international football managers. This article takes a historical and international look at their extraordinary – in many ways unenviable – situation.

The professional football clubs which were formed in Britain during the latter half of the last century and the early decades of this one were run simply by their boards of directors. It was the secretary to the board of a club who acted as go-between for the directors in their dealings with the players. Gradually, however, although the secretaries had no executive power, their responsibility for team matters began to grow, and many were given the title of 'secretary-manager'. While directors continued to pick the team, they were happy for their secretary-managers to travel the country finding players and helping to sign them. They also encouraged a growing public accountability of the secretary-manager, since in many cases they had first-hand experience of the displays of public indignation which invariably greeted a run of poor match results. It became customary for the secretary-manager to resign at the end of such sequences, thus implying a causal connection between the official's departure and the team's low fortunes. This arrangement, whereby the secretary-manager bore ultimate responsibility for the team's performance but lacked executive powers, was steadily eroded between the 1930s and the 1950s. There were several reasons for this. Firstly, the growing wage militancy of professional footballers, combined with their increasing insistence on tactical preparation for matches, persuaded more and more managers that a closer relationship with the team was in their interest. Secondly, the 1930s saw the Football Association, the body ruling English football, beginning to propagate the idea of coaching.

This move took account of the mounting politicization of football, especially in the fascist states of Germany and Italy, and it was aimed primarily to safeguard the international stature of the England team by encouraging coaching at Football League clubs. Early support from within the League for this campaign came from Herbert Chapman, the influential secretary-manager of Arsenal. Men such as Chapman and Frank Buckley of Wolverhampton Wanderers argued for greater efficiency and planning in team matters and for the secretary-manager to be given a free hand in this area. In other countries, football managers were already being established as popular heroes, architects of their teams' successes: in Italy for instance the national victory in the World Cup was widely

attributed to the craft of manager Vittorio Pozzo. Thirdly, in
the period after World War Two, football became a factor in
the newspaper circulation war on Fleet Street. Sports reporters, often required by their editors to provide football stories
on a daily basis, had difficulty getting information from high-
handed directors, and players were prevented by contract
from talking to the press. Increasingly, therefore, football
writers lent their support to League club managers in their
fight for exclusive control of team matters: why, they asked,
didn't the boardroom meddlers take a back seat, and let the
manager manage?

   In the 1950s and 1960s reporting of the football world was
organized increasingly around the figure of the manager.
Match reports now routinely referred to the managers of the
teams involved, while weekday stories focusing on managers'
statements, activity in the transfer market and so on, began to
proliferate. A new gallery of 'team-makers' – Busby, Ramsey,
Shankly, Revie, Nicholson, etc. – was created to stand
alongside pre-war managerial pioneers like Chapman and
Buckley. By the mid-1960s most people knew that Bill Nicholson was manager of Tottenham Hotspur, Matt Busby manager
of Manchester United, Bill Shankly of Liverpool but few
people outside the respective localities knew who had managed Tottenham Hotspur before Nicholson, United before
Busby, or Liverpool before Shankly. By the 1970s, everything
about a team's performance was explained, ultimately, in
terms of the manager. Whatever he did or didn't do, a causal
relationship between him and his club's playing record was
assumed. In 1979, in his book *Diary of A Season*, Lawrie
McMenemy, one of the League's most articulate managers,
reflected that Leeds manager Jimmy Adamson had been
nicknamed Howard Hughes by his players because they never
saw him. Nevertheless, remarked McMenemy, the team had
only lost once in seventeen matches, 'so Jimmy's way must be
right'.

When the England team travelled to Rome to play Italy in
1933, FA Treasurer Arthur Kingscott requested Herbert Chapman to travel with them as unofficial team manager. However,
when Chapman gave the team a pep talk at half time, Kingscott reported him to the FA selection committee for interfer-
ence. This story is recounted by Stanley Rous, who, alone
among FA leaders in the 1930s, perceived the need for English
football to be organized on a more professional basis. Rous
had pioneered annual coaching courses in the 1930s, leading to
the introduction of the FA coaching badge, and in 1946 he secured the appointment of Walter Winterbottom as FA Director
of Coaching and manager of the England team. Winterbottom
had played League football briefly in the 1930s but had then
become a lecturer at the Carnegie College of Physical Education in Leeds. During World War Two, he had been in the Air
Ministry, organizing physical training, and his work there had
impressed Rous.

Winterbottom's appointment seems to have passed almost
unnoticed in the media. Popular press coverage of the 1950
World Cup (the first one entered by England) scarcely mentioned him. The *Daily Herald* of 19 June noted the departure
of 'the (England) party, who also included Mr Walter Winterbottom, team manager. . .'. Thereafter, he received only two
mentions in the *Daily Herald* during the whole tournament –
ordering a three-hour afternoon sleep for the players and, the
following day, visiting the hotel kitchen to ensure that they
could cook British steak and kidney pudding. Stories concentrated on the players. And after England's improbable defeat
by the USA, reporters did not hold the manager responsible.
Clifford Webb wrote in the *Herald*: 'Our failure makes us a
laughing stock – and I'm blaming the players.' In his *Daily
Express* column, John Macadam paid more attention to the
reflections of FA officials like Rous and Arthur Drewry, members of the committee which continued, after all, to select the
team.

If Fleet Street did write about Winterbottom, it was usually to doubt the need for him. The popular press, mindful of the potential prejudice of its readers against 'experts', picked up comments by England players such as Raich Carter and Stanley Matthews which questioned the usefulness of coaching. These apparently veiled criticisms of Winterbottom inspired pressmen to paint a picture of the canny professionals of the England team laughing behind their hands as this alien, professorial figure chalked tactical plans for them on a blackboard – an image fiercely contested by many of the players who actually played for Winterbottom.

The main factors to change Winterbottom's position, albeit obliquely, were the Cold War and the beginnings of Britain's decline. Football became a metaphor for parliamentary democracy and British power. This became clear in 1953 with England's famous defeat at Wembley at the hands of a talented Hungarian team. Before the match there was ambivalence at the *Daily Mirror*. While Bob Ferrier cautiously acknowledged the skill of 'the mighty Magyars', his colleague Peter Wilson called emphatically for an England victory 'because I have visited Hungary and I know how they, like other totalitarian states which I have seen, regard a sporting triumph as a justification for their "superior" way of life.' At the *Daily Express*, Desmond Hackett was confident that the West would prevail: 'Hungary regiments and schemes . . . England can beat Hungary inside ten minutes'. After England's 6–3 defeat, the initial reaction on Fleet Street was respectful of Hungary's skill. Wilson spoke of admiring comments overheard at Wembley, and Hackett, in an all too rare moment of self-mockery, let himself be photographed wearing a dunce's cap. Next day, however, both men were back on the patriotic offensive. Wilson blamed 'the system' whereby club football took precedence over the national side. Hackett talked darkly of 'guilty men', adding that 'we need tough managers who can fire players who slouch in for training'.

The 1954 World Cup found Hackett impatient from the out-
set. In contrast to the restraint of Bob Ferrier, who questioned
Winterbottom politely about the England team's date of arrival in the host country, Switzerland, Hackett presumed to
speak for an increasingly disgruntled populace. He demanded
to know of the FA why it had taken so long to announce the
party. He declared that he was not looking forward to being
once again 'a pallbearer at the funeral of English football'.
Almost inevitably, the competition fed this jingoism. On England's early 2–4 defeat by holders Uruguay, Hackett produced
a maudlin lament: 'This England who made me feel so proud
finally made me weep with frustration. . .'. Once more he pro
nounced the selectors 'the guilty men'.

The following day, all press attention focused on the fracas
at the Hungary–Brazil match, which had apparently involved
players, officials and spectators alike. A senior FA man whom I
interviewed was there, and described it to me as a minor scuf-
fle. The press, however, even though England hadn't been
involved in the match, placed it in the emerging framework of
threats to national pride, about which Something-Must-Be-
Done. It became 'THE BATTLE OF BERNE'. Ferrier, in the *Daily
Mirror*, told how in the stand, 'Brazilian millionaires and their
diamond-dripping senoras stood on their seats screaming for
revenge.' Hackett claimed, unaccountably, to have been
thrown over a fence. To reporters' questions as to whether
England should now leave the tournament, the chairman of FA
selectors Harold Shentall gave the robust reply: 'We taught
them how to play soccer and by gum we'll teach them how to
play the game. Quit? Not blooming likely.' Amid the sound
and fury of BATTLE OF BERNE stories however, *Express*-man
Hackett revealed a new preoccupation: the fact that Gustav
Sebes, manager of England's humiliators, Hungary, was a
'soccer dictator', with full control of team matters.

By 1958 the shrill patriotism which had coloured popular
press reportage of the England team in the early years of the

decade was now the norm. Reporters, undoubtedly conscious
that television was now heightening people's awareness that
the England team was not invincible, now made Winterbottom a more central figure. Headlines told of 'Walter's woe',
'Winterbottom's last chance' and so on. But because Winterbottom didn't officially select the team (he never did, throughout his tenure, although in latter years the committee rubber-
stamped his decisions), press venom concentrated on the FA
selectors, now almost universally portrayed as muddlers and
meddlers.

   In May 1958, while accompanying England on a pre-World
Cup tour, Desmond Hackett fulminated against the FA party
for taking the players cruising on the Danube after a 0–5 defeat
by Yugoslavia: 'What a way to run a World Cup battling soccer
squad. This is more like a kids outing. All they wanted were little fishing nets and a bucket and spade and we would have
been right in the juvenile class which is at the moment our
proper place in international football.' Reporters felt more
confident now to challenge team selections. 'SELECTORS GO
BLUNDERING ON' was Frank McGhee's headline in the *Daily
Mirror* when Bobby Charlton was omitted (thus pre-arranging
a specific ground on which the selectors could be blamed for a
defeat). Sure enough, the selectors were once again branded
'the guilty men' and – another growing feature this – the public
were called as witnesses for the prosecution: 'MIRROR READERS
SAY: SACK OUR SOCCER SELECTORS'.

   The 1962 competition in Chile brought matters to a head. It
was more physical than previous World Cups. Injuries and
sendings-off abounded in the early matches and Stanley Rous,
as president of FIFA, was obliged to appeal for calm. After an
indifferent draw against Bulgaria and a premature exit from
the tournament, McGhee contented himself with an 'I blame
Walter. . .' story, but Hackett was not so easily placated.
Beneath the angry headling 'NO CLASS – THAT'S WHY ENGLAND
FLOPS FLY HOME', he wrote: 'I say Winterbottom's duty is to

stay here and to keep the pathetic little homesick complaining players with him right to the final. They may then appreciate how far down the class of world football they are.' Reflecting on Chile, Rous observed that England had been better 'gentlemen' while other countries had been better 'players'. Winterbottom said simply: 'This was war'. The *Daily Express* listened instead to 'the people'. 'Have YOUR say about England', invited the sports editor.

In August 1962, a *Daily Express* readers' poll named Ipswich manager Alf Ramsey as the popular choice for England team manager. Winterbottom, having failed to get the secretaryship of the FA, departed to the Central Council of Physical Recreation, and in 1963 Ramsey took over. At the time of Ramsey's accession, it was possible to discern three elements – apart from the ability to produce winning teams – in any potentially successful occupant of the England team managership. These were: a full knowledge of coaching and tactics; a background in the professional game (to satisfy the growing sense of professionalism among players); and a preparedness to deal closely with the press, who from now on, since Ramsey was to be the sole selector of the team, would be focusing on Ramsey almost exclusively.

Winterbottom had fulfilled the first and third requirements, being both an internationally respected coach (even when such people were scorned on Fleet Street) and patient and friendly towards reporters. He had never managed a League club, however, nor played much League football, and thus fell foul of the growing ideology of professionalism among League players. With rising salaries for managers, this ideology served, among other things, to preserve managerships for ex-professionals. In the hurly burly of modern professional football, what did men who had 'never played' know? England player Bobby Charlton once suggested that Winterbottom was a chalk-on-his-fingers manager, whereas Ramsey was a mud-on-his-boots manager. The accuracy of this observation (it seems an absurd judgement) matters less than the fact that it was widely believed. Once Winterbottom's assistant, Jimmy Adamson, had indicated his unwillingness to take over, Ramsey was an unbeatable candidate for the England managership in 1962. A former international player of some stature, he had managed unglamorous and far from wealthy Ipswich Town to the League Championship of that year, with a side containing almost no international, or even expensive, players. Here, apparently, was a football manager who could make bricks without straw. Ramsey added to his Svengali image a tetchy and uncommunicative manner, which, by all accounts, he dropped when alone with professional players. Legend has it that, when approached by the Ipswich chairman, anxious to congratulate him on the club's championship success, Ramsey was alone watching a reserve match and replied coldly: 'Do you mind? I'm working.' This unconcealed contempt for 'outsiders' meant that Ramsey's relations with the copy-hungry press corps were never good. But for several reasons, the media treatment of Ramsey, and therefore the public's perception of him, were not as bad as they might have been. Firstly, he appeared to be 'the people's choice'. Secondly, he had a First Division Championship to his credit. Thirdly, his creation of an in-crowd atmosphere among professionals and his surliness with everyone else, inspired a fierce loyalty to him among the England players. Fourthly, most reporters had campaigned for his appointment. Finally, and most importantly, Ramsey (having in 1963 made the prediction, not altogether unique among international team managers, that his team would win the World Cup) found his boast realized a mere three years later – and on home ground at that, with saturation media coverage. This victory earned Ramsey a knighthood and a period of sustained credibility with the press. Media treatment of Ramsey's management was generally supportive, despite his own readiness to prejudice it by reserving most of his thoughts for private discussion with professionals.

Even in 1973, the year before his dismissal, he was prepared, during a tour of Eastern Europe, to insult one of his strongest supporters, Frank McGhee of the *Daily Mirror*, who had asked politely during a press conference why the announcement of the England team would be delayed. 'Do I have to give you reasons?' Ramsey snapped angrily, as McGhee reddened and his colleagues squirmed with embarrassment.

It may have been no accident that, when the FA decided not to appoint Ramsey's successor immediately, they made Joe Mercer caretaker manager. Mercer was a revered and avuncular figure in football, and an ex-England player who had played in both the pre- and post-war eras. In the late 1960s, he had managed Manchester City during a very successful period but had left the club after the team coach Malcolm Allison had claimed to have been the true architect of its success. Mercer's philosophy seemed to belong to those now distant days when 'players just went out and played'. He selected several players of undoubted skill whom Ramsey, with his more functional approach geared to 'work-rate', would have rejected. Trevor Brooking, who played under Mercer, recalls him saying: 'Team talk? What do we want one of those for?'

The virulent populism with which writers like Desmond Hackett afflicted the England selectors in the 1950s (this, incidentally, was not confined to England: an Italian newspaper once ran the headline 'DEATH TO POZZO') has never gone away. It has simply become normal: anyone who managed England in the post-Hackett era could expect from time to time to wake up to headlines of the 'PATHETIC ENGLAND' variety. The manager, convinced on the one hand that he had professional expertise, and on the other that people were right to expect great things from him, accepted this as part of the job. All managers know it simply as 'pressure'. 'Pressure' is something you must live with, but a manager may believe, as Ramsey's permanent replacement Don Revie appeared to believe, that it could be mitigated.

Revie had made his name as manager of Leeds United in the late 1960s. His teams had been successful, but had been unpopular in parts of the football world for what were seen as brutal tactics. However, this appeared not to be a barrier to his appointment. His early moves were often designed to cultivate the press. Reporters appreciated his willingness to provide them with stories and what were soon being called 'traditional' breakfasts of egg and bacon sandwiches. He also accommodated them ideologically, by infusing the England team's affairs with a mawkish patriotism: the honour of playing for England was stressed to players, and English crowds which now grew in number, were issued with *Land of Hope and Glory* songsheets. They were less pleased with the high fees he charged for interviews, which earned him the nickname among the press contingent of 'Don Readies'.

Revie's other credentials were sound: England caps, a proven sense of tactics at top club level and an appreciation of the growing professionalism in all levels of the game. But his sense of his own managerial expertise led him into an absurd paternalism. Before matches, he had the players sitting around playing bingo; he held team meetings where they sat mostly in silence; he issued them with detailed dossiers on the opposition; and he enforced a curfew. He even, on one occasion, suggested they pray to God to make them better players. This was no way to treat proud and affluent professionals: one complained that Revie told the press more than he told the players; another told how the players used the famous dossiers for scribbling down scores in card games.

When Revie left the job in 1977, having negotiated a secret £340,000 agreement to manage the United Arab Emirates football team, the then chairman of the FA, Professor Sir Harold Thompson, spoke of the need for ethics. The managership now passed to Ron Greenwood, a veteran manager and close disciple of Winterbottom in the 1950s. He occasionally resented press intrusions (as, for example, when TV men would grab players for interview after a match abroad, while a satellite transmitter was still in the right position) and the routine criticism that followed a defeat: 'For God's Sake, Pack It In Ron'. Players' biographies from the time of his stewardship reveal affection for Greenwood and respect for his coaching ability, but a feeling that he was 'too nice' for the cut and thrust of modern international football. The press, happy to attribute what were apparently *social* trends in the game (commercialism, defensive and intimidating play,) to an *individual* (Revie), suggested that Greenwood had 'put the smile back on the face of English football'. Greenwood's memoirs, published in 1984, contain an anecdote, the irony of which may have been lost on the author. He describes being a Fulham player in the 1950s and meeting Dugald Livingstone, who came to the club as manager. Livingstone had become known in England when, as manager of lowly Belgium, he had apparently been 'the architect' of a 4–4 draw with England in the 1954 World Cup. Since Belgium had been losing at half-time, Greenwood, as a devotee of coaching, immediately asked Livingstone what he had said to the Belgian players during the interval. Livingstone replied that, since he hadn't the language, he'd simply sat in the corner of the dressing room and sipped a cup of tea.

Greenwood's successor, Bobby Robson, another successful club manager, offered the clearest possibility yet of affirming, through the England managership, the reactionary values of individualism, patriotism and machismo. When he entered the job in 1982, he appealed to England supporters to keep alive 'the spirit of the Falklands'. In his autobiography *Time on the Grass*, he recounts how, after being sacked from the managership of Fulham by club chairman Sir Eric Miller, he had stood in the middle of the Fulham pitch and wept. Years later, when told of Miller's suicide, he had remarked: 'Shows how he stood up to pressure, doesn't it?'

In Britain, the first substantial coverage of the World Cup was
in 1954. By the mid-1960s, the competition was basically a
media event: not only did four hundred million TV viewers
around the world watch the final of 1966, but the wide-ranging
TV coverage obliged other media, such as newspapers, to seek
elsewhere (press conferences, dressing rooms etc.) for stories.
This 'off-the-field' reportage had apparently begun in a small
way in the 1950s and was usually constructed around the
assumption that an anxious and patriotic readership would
wish to know of any lapse in good conduct by their national
representatives. In 1958, an English newspaper disclosed that
England captain Billy Wright was corresponding with Joy
Beverley, a well known singer, who, the paper pointed out,
was married. In 1962, a picture of England player Peter Swan
with a dancing girl, was made to give the impression of dis-
solute behaviour. The implications were clear: if the press
weren't given 'news', they would invent some of their own.
The responsibility for providing 'good news' and preventing
'bad news' inevitably came to lie with the manager.

At the same time, the growth in media attention increased
demands on the manager to produce a winning team. England
failed to qualify for the World Cup finals in either 1974 or
1978. Failure to deliver English participation to the large home
television audience, and therefore to advertisers and sponsors,
lost Ramsey the managership in 1973 and might well have lost
it for Revie four years later, had he not resigned.

In 1978 (as in 1974), Scotland were 'flying the flag' for
British viewers. The team's departure was preceded by a huge
advertisement and publicity campaign: Scottish players
appeared on prime-time TV programmes, were photographed
for numerous advertisements and newspaper stories, and flew
out to an extravagant send off, complete with pipe bands and
drum majorettes. The focal point of the publicity had been the
team manager, Ally MacLeod. From his earliest days in Scottish club management, MacLeod had prided himself on being

able to spot 'quiet days' on the sports pages and to provide reporters with stories that would have maximum impact. The press, he wrote later, 'have a job to do'.

MacLeod received early praise from the media for his 'public relations victories'; his team was dubbed 'ALLY'S TARTAN ARMY'. The trumpeted assessment of MacLeod as a manager was that he was a winner. On TV (as on Fleet Street), news of the World Cup was synonymous with publicity: the Scotland players have arrived in Argentina/the Scottish Squad trained today/the Scottish players are reported to be in good heart/the Scottish team trained again this morning/a Scottish fan has hitch-hiked all the way to Argentina/Scotland supporters have been singing in the streets of Buenos Aires. . . . On 3 June, after months of lucrative myth-making, Scotland were beaten by Peru. Before the game, MacLeod had ritually embraced responsibility for the outcome: 'I have a big mouth and I will take the rap . . . I think that's what I'm paid for.' At half-time, with Scotland down, ITV compere Brian Moore had stared gravely at the camera and observed: 'Not the half-time score we were hoping for.' On BBC-TV, with the game over, Lawrie McMenemy provided a ready explanation (later taken up universally by the media) by asking: 'How many times were Peru watched?' MacLeod, who had only watched Peru play on videotape, now had to explain his apparent lack of preparedness while at the same time coping with a steady stream of allegations by reporters at press conferences that his players were drinking heavily, were out on the town with women and so on. When he moved to restrict the players' movements in their own interests, this was presented in the press as a punishment and thus as validation of the original rumours. When MacLeod suggested that in the Peru match 'we simply did not play well', this became seen as further dereliction on his part: 'MACLEOD: I AM NOT TO BLAME'. One of the Scotland players now failed a dope test and was sent home. That night, a TV camera was sent into a 'morale-boosting' party for the Scottish players and a

reporter attempted to interview the disgraced player, Willie
Johnston. MacLeod's exasperated intervention ('You're
stooping really low now') was taken as evidence that he was
beginning to show the strain. ITN's Trevor MacDonald
reported that night that doubts were now growing about the
competence of the Scotland manager and that, while not yet in
revolt, 'the players don't share his high opinion of himself'.
Meanwhile, a TV camera had been set up outside MacLeod's
home in Scotland and a reporter had offered his 16-year-old
son £25 for an inside story.

On 7 June Scotland's match with Iran was televised. A shot
of MacLeod showed him in the manager's dug-out yelling,
'Come On Archie, Come On!' and punching his palm with his
fist. This drew from BBC commentator John Motson the
remark 'well, they needed that kind of lift a little earlier I
think'. After the match BBC's Jimmy Hill announced that Scotland's manager would now be interviewed, and once again
constructed MacLeod as an incompetent: 'A man who's never
been afraid to come out and face the cameras. Say what you
like about his ability. . .'. MacLeod, during a comparatively
benign interview, now became semi-articulate and rambled: 'I
think you're a man . . . you know what kind of man you are . . .
I think . . . your wife and family . . . when you're happily married . . . Football's a funny game.' Later Lawrie McMenemy
was quick to define success in terms of managers as well: 'The
Argentina manager impresses me. Wherever you go, he's
always taking his notes.' On 8 June, the Scottish *Daily Express*
carried the headline 'THE END OF THE WORLD'. Restaurant own-
ers in Scotland put up signs reading 'Ally MacLeod does NOT
eat here.' A representative of Chrysler, whose cars had been
advertised by the Scotland squad, appeared on television to
say that he didn't think that sales would be adversely affected
by the team's misfortunes: the Avenger was, he said, 'still a
good car'. Scotland players had meanwhile begun to sell
'stories' to the popular press. They included one by Don Mas-

son, in the *Sun* ('MY SHAME', 8 June), in which he claimed to have taken the same drug as the banished Johnston. Mac-Leod's future became a major talking point. On 11 June, McMenemy stated on BBC-TV that the press could not be blamed for recent attacks on MacLeod. He maintained, somewhat bizarrely, that: 'It's their job to write sensationalism. It's their job to report facts.' The following day, after Scotland had gained their only victory (against Holland, the eventual runners-up) with a changed line-up, MacLeod's many critics now had further ammunition. Why hadn't he picked this 'winning combination' before? There was, however, no possible way of knowing that this team would have done as well, against Peru *or* Iran, or that the team which played in the first two games would *not* have played as well against Holland as the one that was fielded.

On his return to Scotland, MacLeod narrowly avoided dismissal. When he had selected his squad for the next international match, he asked his employers, the Scottish FA, whether he was obliged by his contract to hold a press conference. When told that he wasn't, he didn't hold one. Several newspapers, confident as ever in their role of Voices of the People, said he had spurned the fans.

More than ever, the modern sports media create social worlds, and events, while claiming only to observe them. In Britain, it is the preferred belief that it is only in Eastern European countries that play is 'regimented', and only in 'banana republics' or Latin American dictatorships that rabble-rousing TV commentators shriek, 'Goooooooooooal!' and team managers are dismissed every few months. Before the 1978 final, for example, ITN's Trevor MacDonald portrayed Argentine manager César Luis Menotti as a nervous chain smoker in a country where 'football is a *religion*, where winning is the *only* thing that matters and where the job of the football manager is *notoriously precarious*'. Indeed, the World Cup of recent times has been a relentlessly self-referring affair for the media, with football people being described as much in terms of their relationship with the media as anything else.

If the World Cup were to be awarded to the players who can give interviews in the most languages, Tony Gubba told BBC1 viewers on 24 June 1978, then the Dutch would already be champions. To ITV's Brian Moore, however, the Dutch manager was 'a strange man . . . that doesn't talk to press or television.' (21 June 1978) In the 1982 finals, Jim Rosenthal, in Madrid for ITV, asked England manager Ron Greenwood if he had made any changes in the team for the West Germany match. Greenwood, sometimes cagey with the media and resentful on occasion of criticism by studio panels, smiled: 'You'd have a birthday if I did wouldn't you? You lot? You and your panel back there?' Was the tension getting to Greenwood, mused Brian Moore, back in London.

Manchester City manager John Bond said he couldn't understand why Greenwood was so sensitive; Jimmy Greaves (briefly a player under Greenwood at West Ham) commented that 'Ron was apt to panic'; and Brian Clough, the manager of Nottingham Forest, was contemptuous. 'A few years ago,' he said of Greenwood, 'he wasn't good enough to be on a panel.' Thus Clough, the professional football man, now spoke *for television*, implying TV football punditry to be a higher accolade for which success in the football world itself was only one prerequisite.

It should not be forgotten that this half crazy process through which managerial reputations are built and destroyed is real in its consequences. Many managers are brought near to mental breaking point. At the time of the last World Cup, the Yugoslavian manager, Miljan Miljanic commented: 'Football coaches are being subjected to a kind of terrorism by the press and TV. It has become almost impossible to do the job.' Claudio Coutinho, manager of Brazil, said: 'It is intolerable. When we lost last week in France my family could hardly leave the house back home in Rio. Life was impossible for my ten-year-old son at school.' And former manager of West Germany, Helmut Schoen, put it most eloquently: 'The World Cups of 1958 and 1962 were garden parties compared with what is involved now . . . in nearly all countries of the world, football is the most popular sport. Today the media bring it to the masses and bring the feelings and demands of the masses back to those working in the game. Football has become almost a kind of war.' 'And,' he concluded, 'success has many fathers, defeat only one.'

4. YOU'VE REALLY GOT A HOLD ON ME: FOOTBALLERS IN THE MARKET

Steve Redhead

This piece looks at how, over the last twenty years, the World Cup has become the lynch-pin of a series of international labour markets in professional footballers. It concentrates on the problems created for the English Professional Footballers' Association (PFA), which has become identified with the campaign for 'freedom of contract' and yet simultaneously fights strongly for import controls on 'foreign' players. The implications of the PFA experience for other player associations are by no means clear – given different national and inter-continental policies, histories, team styles, and so on – but no one interested in future trade union struggles can afford to ignore them.

In the early 1960s, Jimmy Hill wrote in what turned out to be rather a premature autobiography:

> I would like to say this in a general way to all chairmen and directors of football clubs in England. I think if there is a general fault on your side it is that you tend to live in the age of the Industrial Revolution, with a master-and-man attitude. Some of you are beginning to realize that that age is over; even if it were not, it is difficult to treat professional footballers as one does ordinary employees.

The book, *Striking For Soccer* – an ironic title, since Hill never scored many goals and there had in fact been no strike – gives an account of the Professional Footballers' Association (the

Players' Union prior to 1958) involvement in the abolition of the maximum wage in 1961. Not long after it was published, the players had seemingly even more to celebrate, though Hill had already moved on, and up, into football management at Coventry City, from whence he launched into an even more successful career in television. In 1963, after he had been transferred to Arsenal, George Eastham eventually won a High Court declaration against his former club, Newcastle United. The ruling was that the retain and transfer system which had operated since before the turn of the century was illegal. These two events – abolition of the maximum wage and the outlawing of retain and transfer – were taken to signify a qualitatively new era in professional soccer.

For many in English League soccer, Hill's words rang true: these years really did mark a watershed. Soccer 'slavery' had been replaced by 'freedom': at a stroke, or perhaps two, the great twin shackles of wage restriction and retention clauses had apparently been severed for good. By the early 1970s, academics like G.W. Keeton, a Professor of Law, could write about the 'football revolution' and colour supplement journalist Hunter Davies was spending a year in observation of the newly affluent footballers of Spurs. The long-shorted, big-booted heroes of yesteryear were dead and buried; the forward march of sporting labour was not to be halted. Or so the story goes.

There is certainly no doubt that what happened to professional footballers in the 1960s – their legal 'rights', their pay packets and even their hairstyles – was important. The period of the late 1950s through to the mid-1960s witnessed what, in some respects, was the football industry's most successful assertion of trade union power on behalf of its major employees, the players. But one should not get carried away. The PFA may have been moving away from serfdom under the likes of Jimmy Hill and the long-serving secretary, Cliff Lloyd, but it was always a very limited conception of 'freedom' which

beckoned from over the horizon. Lloyd, for instance, shortly
before his retirement in the 1980s, reiterated his belief that the
'transfer system will *always* be there in football'.

Just as some of the origins of Britain's present economic
crisis might be said to lie in the (lack of a) seventeenth-century
revolution, football's current malaise in its mother country in
part stems from the failure to break the chains of its 'glorious'
past. Football feudalism may indeed have died a death on the
battlefields of the Ministry of Labour and the High Court in
1961 and 1963 respectively, but its corpse kept writhing long
enough for 'freedom of contract' to be blamed for soccer's
crisis in the late 1970s and 1980s and for the resurrection of a
maximum wage to be seen as a 'realistic' strategy for many
boards of directors and managers once the banks started to
close their doors to clubs. It may well be that, as former 'failed'
footballer, Fred Eyre, has put it, 'since the days when
Fulham's inside forward Jimmy Hill led the players out of . . .
poverty to guzzle milk and honey in the promised land, the
footballer is looked upon in a different light by the supporter.'
But many part-and full-time professionals continue, in the
days of millionaire superstardom for some at home and
abroad, to earn paltry wages and are subjected to disciplinary
regimes which would make most fans riot.

If the George Eastham case in the 1960s (and a later 1970s
testing of the same issues internationally) constituted symbolic
victory for the soccer serfs against their masters, a European
Court decision in 1976 was to have a more profound impact in
the long run. The Court's judgement ruled that the Italian
Football Federation was in breach of certain Articles of the
Treaty of Rome by normally granting permission to play professional soccer only to Italian nationals; a ban on imports in
effect, disqualifying 'foreign' footballers from acting as professionals for Italian clubs. An earlier European Court case on
cycling in 1974 had already established that European
Economic Community (EEC) law prohibited any discrimina-

tion based on nationality in professional/semi-professional sport. Freedom of movement for citizens of countries within the EEC was proclaimed by these two legal decisions to override the autonomy of national football associations of member states. However, the judgement was initially flagrantly disregarded in Italy and it took a meeting in Brussels in 1978 between the European Union of Football Associations (UEFA) and the EEC Commission to produce a working agreement which, while recognizing the decision to outlaw national discrimination against the employment of footballers from other EEC countries, provided that clubs could in the short term limit their intake to two non-nationals. The revised regulations issued by UEFA in 1978 to cover the movement of players between EEC-nation clubs still envisaged, of course, that there would be a transfer system in operation. The rules laid down that players were free to move to any club in the EEC on expiry of their contract, but that in the event of two clubs failing to agree on the size of a transfer fee there would be, after 30 days, a decision by a 'Board of Experts' (similar to the system introduced in England in the same year when the PFA won its modified 'freedom of contract' claim).

The influx of the world's top players into Italy following the national team's triumph in the World Cup final in Spain in 1982 – both from inside and outside the EEC – led eventually to a further Italian ban on 'imports', but the whole structure of European football – and possibly of soccer throughout the world – is on the brink of major change if the Common Market does in fact implement in full the European Court's decision. The eventual end of national restrictions – at least for the EEC – is on the cards for the beginning of the 1986–7 season. In 1984, Football League secretary Graham Kelly, along with other representatives of national associations and UEFA, met the Common Market Commissioner to stave off the 'evil' day when players within the EEC would for the first time be fully 'free agents'. After the meeting, which secured an agreement to postpone for a year the ending of restrictions (originally designed to start in the 1985–6 season), Kelly claimed:

> We now know we can fight only a stonewall action. But we will eventually have to come into line. We are against abandoning restrictions entirely because of the effects that would have at both club and international level. It would put us at a disadvantage against clubs from outside the Market and could dilute the quality of international teams.

These anxieties were underscored by Gordon Taylor, Cliff Lloyd's successor as secretary of the PFA, who commented that:

> Our biggest worry if the restrictions are lifted is that our best players will be snapped up abroad and be replaced by cheaper inferior foreign players. The Italian clubs would be delighted if the rules are changed. We could be saying goodbye to players like Ian Rush and Bryan Robson. Some clubs abroad seem to talk in monopoly money – how could our clubs resist some of the phenomenal offers they're bound to get? It would be easy for a trickle to become a flood.

The PFA support for the League's stance came as no surprise. For several years before this temporary reprieve was granted, the union had been campaigning for an end to the import of all but 'top class' players from non-EEC countries. PFA support for Department of Employment regulation of work permits to Polish, Yugoslav, Argentinian and other 'foreign' players had grown since the 1978 World Cup finals in Argentina when the sight of players such as Ardiles, Villa, Tarantini and so on persuaded a few dour British managers that they were behind the times. The response – from terrace and dressing room alike – to such 'immigration' of World Cup talent into British football was always ambivalent, reaching a climax with the reception meted out to Ardiles around the time of the Falklands War.

By 1981, many 1978 World Cup stars had already come and gone from view, one of the peculiarities of English League football which must have bemused them almost as much as it did the fans. Kaziu Deyna's experience at Manchester City was salutary. Pilloried in his own country for missing a penalty in the finals, his arrival at Maine Road prompted great expectations. The idea that East European team styles were dour was fast disappearing, and Poland were clearly a force to be reckoned with. To see this World Cup skipper flounder in the mud of mid-winter League matches was almost beyond belief. At that time, City were still one of the top English sides. But Malcolm Allison was soon to be exposed as the returning Emperor with no clothes, and perhaps Deyna's obvious astonishment that his team-mates could not read his acutely intelligent passes, or trap the ball instantly, and yet insisted on running for ninety minutes, was simply foresight that the Football League was doomed.

Nevertheless, by this time, the PFA were pressing really hard for only 'established international professional players' to be allowed into the country from non-EEC states, and were fighting for even tighter controls. Their aim was that 'no player over 28' should be hired, and that they 'should have gained six caps for their countries in the last three years'. Gordon Taylor stated at the time: 'We are not the only country to be thinking on these lines. Five million pounds' worth of players have come into this country, and thirty out of fifty have not made the grade.' Such anti-free-trade-in-footballers arguments sit uneasily alongside the union's long struggle for 'freedom of contract' nationally and internationally, and the players' association came under strident criticism for its 'protectionism'.

However, its position was more complicated than it seemed at first sight. The 'import controls' policy had gone hand in hand with a consistent criticism of the transfer system, and the overriding aim remained to replace the inflation-ridden format which prevailed in the late 1970s with an 'Italian' style compensation mechanism. Under this, fees for players would be based on age, experience, status of previous club and former salary. In the event, the great transfer crash of the early 1980s merely proved the union's general argument – that the valuation of players' labour power was massively exaggerated for current market conditions. Laurie Madden, then with Charlton Athletic, responded to an attack on the 'protectionist' outlook of the union in *Marxism Today* by admitting that: 'I think personally that the PFA has been co-opted into a management philosophy by its over determined bid to become "acceptable" bargaining partners. . .' He also predicted (accurately, as it turned out) the widening gap between the (very few) rich clubs and the rest, and the likely long term consequences for the vast majority of the PFA's membership. In this context, Madden argued, the union's role *was* to limit overseas players' rights:

> The PFA are not against Ardiles and company. They are concerned that this may have detrimental effects on the game. Large sums of money are going out of the game. Secondly, if there is an influx of South American players to this country it would mean less opportunity for youngsters coming into the game. Thirdly, it is possible that the international side could suffer. Italy seems to be of the same opinion.

Things have been difficult for the PFA. On the one hand, since the early 1980s it has been helping to bail out bankrupt clubs almost weekly so that its members could be paid. On the other it has had to avoid an apparent identity of interests with the employers. The fervour for import controls on footballers also found its way onto the sports pages of Mrs Thatcher's flagship, the *Daily Mail*. The paper purred with pleasure in March 1981 as it slapped a headline announcing a 'Curb Soon on Cheap Foreign Imports', over an article referring to continuing attempts by PFA and government to 'stem the tide'. The *Mail*'s choice of language – 'the English players' union worried that the signing of *overseas* players was threatening their already *overcrowded* profession' and a '*flood* of cheap foreign imports' (my emphasis) – had distinct echoes of Powellite speeches on race in the 1960s and 1970s. It also recalled the prime minister's own pre-election comments on the 'swamping' of our culture when she was leader of the opposition.

The way that such chauvinistic sentiments have been expressed in the football world laid the basis for a much sharper expression of 'patriotic' feeling regarding the 1982 World Cup finals in Spain. At this time, Britain was at war with Argentina over the Falklands. Right up to the opening of the competition, the players of Scotland, Northern Ireland and England agonized over whether to withdraw because of Argentina's presence. In early May, Kevin Keegan, then England's captain, stated his view:

> Morally, the way the situation is, we cannot go and play the Argentines. We earn our living in this country and live by its laws and if the government says we don't go, that is it. I personally would not have any qualms about obeying what the government says. We cannot expect our lads to go out to the Falklands and be killed as they were on HMS Sheffield and then have to face Argentina in two months' time at football. There is no way we can do it. It would be hypocritical. But . . . it is not up to the players.

Trevor Brooking, then Keegan's lieutenant in the England side, agreed with this mixture of uncritical nationalistic passion and humble deference: 'It's up to the government. We want to go but it's not up to us . . . if it comes to it, and the gov-

ernment advises the FA not to go, then we have to accept it.'
Alan Gowling, then chairman of the PFA, weighed in with a
more cautious rhetoric, but he still backed the line that 'if the
government tells us not to go, then obviously we will support
the government', It was left to Harry Lawrie, secretary of the
Scottish PFA, unequivocally to urge withdrawal: 'We are not
prepared to sit back and even consider participating in a tournament with a country which has killed our brothers.'

The process of once again moulding British working-class
opinion to a colonial adventure was as manifest in Spain in
1982 as it was in Britain, during the South Atlantic campaign
and in the build up to the 1983 General Election. Who could
expect football and footballers to be exempt? The old adage
about there not being many radical soccer players was high-
lighted yet again when, very shortly after the ending of the
1982 World Cup, Jimmy Hill, the old campaigner for 'freedom', was defying a FIFA ban on sporting relations with South
Africa by spearheading a 'rebel' tour involving World Cup
players from Argentina alongside English, Dutch, Belgian and
Brazilian professionals. Before the 'pirates' came home in disgrace Hill defended his participation on the basis of players'
rights, just as he had in *Striking For Soccer* twenty years previously. He claimed in July 1982 that:

> I've been banned before! Sometimes, to establish a
> principle, you have to go through a bit of trouble. I've done
> that before in my life. . . . If the players are banned my view
> is that they will win hands down in the courts because of the
> restraint of trade law but no one wants it to come to that.

Not all PFA officials have been as reactionary as Jimmy Hill.
The union has had a number of 'soccer rebels' in its ranks over
the years, but the names of Billy Meredith, Charlie Roberts
and Jimmy Guthrie recall earlier eras of the game's history.
Since the early 1960s, it has been a 'different ball game' for

trade unionism in the football industry. A number of players – Hill, Terry Neill, Derek Dougan – have initially made their names as chairmen of the PFA before becoming 'establishment' figures within the industry, but there are many more who have selflessly given the same service to their fellow professionals as they formerly gave to their clubs. The failings of union strategy cannot be pinned on the door of a few careerists.

The problem for the PFA – and all team-sports player associations throughout the world, for the matter – is that it is impossible to create 'freedom of contract' in only one country. The paternalistic football culture inherited from so many years of retain and transfer has mixed with a refusal to accept the widening gap between League football and the European and South American standards of play (and consequently the gulf between British international soccer and *both* the World's premier stylists like France, Italy, Brazil, Argentina *and* the 'emerging' nations). These elements catch the 'freedom fighters' of the PFA in a dangerous double bind. Who really believes the PFA's claim that 'continental' imports are 'inferior' to the vast majority of journeymen professionals now covering every inch of the park twice a week throughout the season? Preserving jobs in the industry is all well and good but not if the price is the misplaced and dated chauvinism that is echoed every time an England manager opens his mouth. Alf Ramsey's 'animals' jibe at the 1966 Argentinian World Cup party was the equivalent of the *Sun*'s 'Gotcha' jingoism in 1982.

There is also a more specific pitfall for the players' union. The irony of a government supposedly committed to the liberation of market forces collaborating gleefully with a trade union in order to regulate 'freedom of movement' from within and without the EEC is striking. But it is entirely in keeping with neo-liberal thinking in the economics of sport to argue for labour market controls over sportsmen in general and professional footballers in particular. In football, club and League officials have always argued that labour market controls are necessary for the survival of the sport. A pamphlet from the Institute for Economic Affairs (IEA), published in 1980 and called, unashamedly, *Sport in the Market* singled out professional sports as industries to be exempted from monopoly and restrictive practices law, as in the United States of America, where the reserve clause (similar to the retain and transfer restrictions) has prevailed despite general legislative intervention against other forms of 'restraint of trade'. Neo-liberalism, in sports especially, makes a point of stopping short of calling for the total abolition of labour market controls. No wonder the *Daily Mail* welcomed the PFA opposition to 'blue collar' foreign footballing imports!

What, then, is to be done? Unquestionably, the notion of professional footballers having 'rights' to 'freedom' have taken on a distinctly right-wing inflexion in recent years. I have argued that this is not simply because most professional soccer players would back Reaganite/Thatcherite 'liberalism' till the cows come home. The reason lies as much with the transfer system. It remains pervasive in its influence, despite the modifications of the 1960s and 1970s, and provides footballers and their representative associations with very little room for man-oeuvre. Even the richest of the superstars – Maradona and company – due to take the field in Mexico this summer will find it hard to escape the feeling of being a male model selling his wares to the highest bidder. A world market in footballers without a transfer system would of course necessitate a giant leap in the imagination of football's governing bodies and the representatives of its collective workforce. No one in the game has really come to grips with what constitutes 'freedom' from labour market controls for professional footballers, although this has been the supposed goal of its workers' organizations since the apparent liberation of the player prior to the World Cup in 1966.

Football badly needs its players to give a lead – as cricketers like Ian Botham, Viv Richards and Clive Lloyd have in opposition to 'freedom' to tour South Africa – but the industry itself is cowed and frightened in the wake of the Brussels and Bradford disasters: conservatism plus crisis equals more conservatism. Yet the PFA *has* shown itself opposed to unchained market forces in football – albeit misguidedly in the case of 'imports' – and it should not be beyond its members to devise strategies for intervention in professional soccer's marketplace. To counter its isolation at home (and heavy dependence on League funds for its activities) it could strengthen present ties abroad with other player associations, through its membership of the Federation Internationale des Footballeurs Professionels (FIFPRO), a grouping of sports player associations committed to full freedom of contract. The PFA has long pursued a lone path, separate from the wider trade union and labour movement, exacerbated by its willingness to register under the Industrial Relations Act of 1971. It is fiercely opposed to amalgamations with other trade unions, an option which the Scottish PFA took up in 1975 when it joined forces with what is now the General, Municipal, Boilermakers and Allied Trades Union (GMBATU). But as a result it has too often had to resort to legal routes to 'freedom'. The clash of PFA objectives and EEC law is only the latest example of the precarious nature of this route. Articulate PFA advocates of players' rights in recent years – such as Gordon Taylor, Alan Gowling, Steve Coppell – have been acutely aware of the problems facing the organization without being able to set a new course which embraces 'freedom of movement' within the EEC *and* the defence of hard won rights at home.

The 1986 World Cup may well be the last before the EEC countries – soon to include Spain and Portugal – throw their doors open to all comers. The stage is set for a major free-for-all in the world transfer market in professional footballers. Buyers and sellers all over the world will be programming their videos so that they can record the skills of the 'new Maradonas' who will emerge as the most marketable commodities from this year's competition. Players like Maradona, Zico, Socrates and so on could probably tell the new stars a thing or two about the dark side of World Cup cattle markets after their experiences in Spain and Italy since the last competition. But will they listen?

Bibliography

G.W. Keeton *The Football Revolution: A Study of the Changing Pattern of Association Football* Newton Abbott: David & Charles, 1972

H. Davies *The Glory Game* New edition, with an updated introduction, Sphere Books 1985

F. Eyre *Another Breath of Fred Eyre* Glossop: Senior Publications, 1982

P. Sloane 'Sport in the Market? The Economic Causes and Consequences of The 'Packer Revolution' Hobart Paper No 85, Institute of Economic Affairs, 1980

Court Cases:

Eastham v Newcastle United and others (1964) Ch.413

Cooke v Football Association (1972) The *Times*, 24 March 1972

Gaetano Dona v Mario Mantero, Case 13/76 (1976) ECR 1333

Walrave v Union Cycliste Internationale, Case 36/74 (1974) ECR 1405

5. SOME ENGLISHMEN AND SCOTSMEN ABROAD: THE SPREAD OF WORLD FOOTBALL

Tony Mason

> Everton have been invited to take their team over to
> Holland by the Football Association. They are to meet
> another first-class English club as a sort of education for the
> Continentals. . . .
>
> Everton match programme, April 17, 1908

When the First World War broke out in 1914, the Corinthians,
the leading amateur football team in Britain, were on their
way to South America to play a series of football matches for
the fourth time in five years. News of the start of the war
reached their ship, and on arrival in Rio they paused only to re-
coal before turning straight back. An Italian team which
arrived in Brazil shortly after spent a year there until they felt
able to return. Several British coaches were taken unawares by
the pace of events and interned in Germany for the duration.
The trivial consequences of war, perhaps, but they offer some
indication of the extent of football's empire. By 1914, the
game already appeared set to take over the world. It had not
only become a rival to the 'insidious coffee house atmosphere
of Hungary', as one Corinthian wrote, but it had even been
adopted by the German Army, because of the improvements
in physique and solidarity it was supposed to promote.

From Calais to the Urals, Helsinki to Genoa, football was
being played to an increasingly sophisticated standard. And
the feet of the English were everywhere, playing the game in
their schools, playing it among themselves in the adult world

outside, both in general clubs and in clubs specifically founded
for the purpose, and playing it in factories and railway yards.
British soldiers carried footballs in their knapsacks and British
sailors tucked them in their kitbags. British teams and British
coaches were in demand all over Europe and beyond. In what
follows I want to give some indication of the pattern and tex-
ture of this process, to show what happened and how it happened, and in particular to mark the spread of the game to
Europe and South America. But I also want to examine why,
by the time of the first World Cup in 1930, significant areas of
the world seemed relatively undeveloped so far as football was
concerned: notably Australia, India, South Africa and North
America.

Of course, the British were not the only force behind the
spread of football. Every country had its indigenous
enthusiasts both on and off the field. The British were important because they were a prestigious world power who had
pioneered a simple, attractive and manly game. Britain's man-
ufacturing and trading power took British sales reps,
engineers, bankers, managers, clerks and manual workers to
all parts of the world. It was apparently English engineers who
introduced the game to Bilbao in 1893. The first effective
teams in Rumania were, according to the *Times*, organized by
British workers at the Colentina textile factories and the
Ploesti Standard Oil fields. It was an English entrepreneur
who awarded a cup which was competed for by local teams in
St Petersburg between 1907 and 1917. The Genoa Cricket and
Athletic Club was founded in 1893 by English port employees
and soon renamed the Football and Athletic Club; in 1897 it
was agreed to admit Italians as members. One of the first ever
football matches played in Brazil was between the two British
teams of the English Gas Company and the São Paulo Rail-
ways in São Paulo in 1895. Motives were obviously mixed. But
the Charnock family, who introduced the game to their textile
workforce in Morozovsky 60 miles from Moscow in the 1890s,

clearly loved the game and one of them at least was a formid-
able player. They had been reared in Lancashire, where the
English professional game had exploded in the 1880s. Doubtless they hoped football would help to keep their workers
attached and loyal. But it was also a game they enjoyed playing
themselves. It was that enjoyment which probably led the four
British workmen in the Uruguayan Central Railway Shops in
Montevideo to found a team which, under the name Penarol,
was able to welcome exalted visitors from Nottingham Forest
in 1904. And the connections of commerce could also run in
the other direction. Eduardo Bosio, a salesman in optical
goods from Turin, travelled a lot in England. He formed a
team among his employees in 1891.

Contacts made through commerce are sometimes transitory. But they often led to permanent settlement, frequently
of significant numbers of people. By 1877, more than 30,000
British nationals lived in Buenos Aires province, and a steady
flow of British immigrants continued into the twentieth century, as a result of the large amounts of British capital invested
in Argentina. Settlement was accompanied by schools such as
that founded in Buenos Aires in 1884 by Alexander Watson
Hutton. This Scotsman included football in his curriculum,
and it was not long before a dozen clubs had been established
in the Argentinian capital, mostly with British membership.
By 1893, Hutton was President of the Argentinian FA and the
English High School was an early winner of the championship.
After 1900, though, the game was increasingly in Argentinian
hands.

English schools and colleges in St Petersburg were already
playing football by the end of the 1890s, and English schools
like the one at Neuwied am Rhein helped to introduce the
game to Germany. Young Englishmen sent to Swiss schools in
the 1880s took football with them. The Lausanne Cricket and
Football Club was exclusively British, and showed it by refus-
ing to play on Sundays. The Zürich Grasshoppers were an

English foundation. When the Swiss Football Association was founded in 1895, the Vice-President and most of the delegates were English. Further afield, football was taught in the Gordon Memorial College in Khartoum, and the Marist Colleges and the English Mission Schools in South Africa and India. The role of the school could also operate in reverse. After a stay in England, Konrad Koch introduced football into recreational afternoons at his Gymnasium in Braunschweig in 1874. Señor Guissasola, President of Reál Gijon in 1921, had learned his football at Richmond Hill School. Finally, as is well known, Baron Pierre de Coubertin and other enthusiasts promoted the spread of 'English' games in France in the hope that they would produce an elite similar to that produced by the English public schools. This elite, they hoped, would bridge the gap between the aristocracy and the bourgeois and would stand up to the Germans.

Such communities found exclusiveness difficult to maintain and favoured locals would soon be allowed to share in the sport. Mixed teams might turn out against British visitors, like the mixed English and Austrian eleven which lost 13–0 to Oxford University in 1899. By 1900, teams of foreign residents were playing teams of Russians in St Petersburg, a prelude to the formation of a local league in 1901. By 1908, the Russian clubs were getting the better of the local British ones but were as yet no match for visitors. It was the experience of the British players which made them so valuable. When Racing Club de Paris entertained Richmond Town Wanderers in 1906, they fielded but four Frenchmen alongside three Swiss and four Englishmen. Clearly, once the locals had taken up the game in earnest the English residents could not hope to hold their own, but the process often took twenty years. In 1900, English clubs in Uruguay were as good as anyone: by the 1920s there was no such club and Uruguay had already won a South American championship. Only in countries of the Empire such as Canada and India were English residents or recent immigrants

able to maintain a dominant position in local football after
World War One. Was it nostalgia that prompted the European
players in both countries to stage their own England v Scotland
internationals?

While commerce and education were the two most important channels by which football was transmitted to other countries the role of the British armed forces should not be forgotten. Teams from visiting British warships played in Montevideo. HMS Amethyst put out a team against Fluminense in
Rio in 1906, and six years later the visit of British sailors to São
Paulo allegedly led to the formation of Santos. One of the first
games to be played in Barcelona, in 1898, was against a team of
British sailors and the Navy even played the locals in Tirana in
1925. Football's revival in Turkey after World War One was
partly the result of the activities of occupying British soldiers
and sailors But the Army probably had its most significant
impact in India and South Africa. I shall return to consider
these countries in more detail later; suffice to note here that 49
British regiments entered the Durban football competition in
1911. One of the unlooked for, and few, benefits of the First
World War was the spread of football, as French peasants
from remote parts of France were introduced to the game in
their battalions and Austrian POWs contributed to a raising of
footballing standards in Russia.

But if it was often the British resident, the migrant worker,
the teacher and the profit-seeker who were the first to run after
footballs exported from Gamages or Lillywhites, it was the
British touring team and the British football coach who consolidated the game's position. The touring team showed what
could be achieved and the coach came to help the local players
achieve it. British football teams went everywhere in the years
1900–14. The south of England, with its proximity to the continent and its many amateur teams staffed by young men not
short of a bob or two, sent many sides abroad, especially at
Easter and in the early summer. For club members, touring

became a regular attraction in which football, seeing the sights, and socializing with your side and theirs were of equal importance. Richmond Old Boys, based on the Richmond County School, was made up of young men from the worlds of business and academia. A goalkeeping Frenchman had the contacts, and a tour fund, into which each member contributed a few shillings a week, covered the cost of four days in France – about £3 per head. Matchés were played in Calais, Lille and Roubaix in 1901 and all were won handsomely. After that, invitations came flooding in. In order to give the team selectors more scope, its name was changed to Richmond Town Wanderers in 1905. In 1912 it was changed again, and for a very significant reason. The standard of football in Europe had improved so much that club officials realized that in order to maintain the team's playing success, it would have to be strengthened by choosing from a much wider area. Hence the birth of Middlesex Wanderers, who from 1912 to 1931 came together only in order to take the best of British amateur football to the foreigner. But perhaps not quite the best. For the aristocrats of the amateur game were the Corinthians.

The Corinthians had been founded in 1882 in an attempt to produce in England the superior teamwork thought to be the chief factor in Scotland's superiority in the annual international match. The Corinthians, composed of ex-public schoolboys and university men, became the standard-bearers of the amateur tradition and were capable of holding their own with the professionals right up to the First World War. They too were inveterate tourers. Their first tour was to South Africa in 1897, and they went again in 1903 and 1907. They went to Canada and the United States in 1906, 1911 and 1924 and Brazil in 1910, 1913 and 1914. European visits were commonplace after the first trips to Hungary and Scandinavia in 1904. It took the best part of three weeks just to get to South Africa or South America in those days. Time and money were needed for such jaunts and this team of students and public school masters was not short of either, especially before 1914. Their importance in helping to advance football in those places they visited should not be underestimated. In São Paulo there still exists a first-class club called Corinthians. After visits to Hungary and Sweden, they offered a cup to be competed for by local amateur teams. Everywhere they went, they were feted by large crowds and given a social reception befitting their status as English sporting gentlemen. The social arrangements occasionally proved inappropriate. Half-time during a match in Geneva in 1909 lasted three-quarters of an hour and included a large meal.

But by 1900 it was the British professional game that was to the forefront in setting standards at home, and professional teams were also touring abroad. Southampton, Nottingham Forest, Everton and Tottenham, even Southern Leaguers Swindon and Exeter, had all been to Argentina before the outbreak of war in 1914. Everton made a profit of £300 from their five-match, two-week tour in 1909. Two of the matches were exhibitions against Tottenham. The same two clubs had met in Vienna and Prague in 1905. Burnley and Liverpool carried on the tradition in Milan in 1922. Sometimes quite elaborate tournaments were held, like the Vienna Festival of Sport in 1912 when Tottenham, Arsenal, Ajax, Victoria Berlin, Vienna FC, Rapide Vienna and Middlesex Wanderers competed and Vienna beat the Wanderers 5–0 in the final. Representative tours before 1914 were rarer and inevitably depended on private enthusiasm. The visit of a mixed amateur and professional Football Association team to Germany in 1899 would not have taken place if a German enthusiast, Ivo Schricker, had not persuaded his mother to put up the £200 needed to meet expenses.

Tours were important not simply as a means of demonstrating skills and tactics on the field, but also in gaining the patronage of those elites who were probably crucial to the progress of football, especially in its early stages. The president of Argen-

tina was present when Everton played Tottenham in 1909, as
was the president of Brazil, the following year, when the
Corinthians played in São Paulo. The crown prince and prin-
cess saw Newcastle United play in Berlin in 1909, and all this
before an English king had even attended a Cup Final.

Middlesex Wanderers were once billed in Sweden as 'middle class wanderers', and with the exception of the professionals, the bulk of our football tourists were middle class right
enough. But the exception is an important one and includes
one small group of British working men whose influence on
the progress of football outside their own country was dispro-
portionate to their small numbers. Because if British teams
were in demand, so were British coaches. They were to be
found everywhere, from Spain to Hungary, to Italy and
Uruguay. In particular, the Scots footballer turned coach was
as ubiquitous as the Scots engineer – men like John Hurley,
John Dick and Henry Madden, the latter managing Slavia
Prague from 1905 to 1938.

Jimmy Hogan was perhaps the most outstanding example,
made more so by the fact that in spite of his record overseas he
was a prophet with little honour in his own country. He first
toured Holland as a player with Bolton Wanderers in 1909,
and about eighteen months later accepted a coaching job
there. He was appointed coach to the Dutch international eleven, and in 1912 took a two month engagement to prepare the
Austrian team for that year's Olympics. While in Vienna he
also coached some of the local club sides. He worked in
Europe from 1918 to 1934, in Austria, Hungary, Germany,
France, Holland and Switzerland; he coached the Austrian XI
who reached the Olympic Final in 1936; and he was closely
associated with the Wunder Mannschaft which did so well in
the 1930s. That in itself was a sign of how deep British influence had gone.

Europe and Latin America had been captivated by the
British game, even if they quickly developed their own way of

playing it. But what of those countries over which Britain had exercised imperial authority – Australia, South Africa and India, for example? Why had not football taken off there? And why had it not taken off in the United States of America and Canada, where so many emigre British men and women now lived?

Of course much depends on what you mean by football 'taking off'. Certainly the game was played more or less extensively in all those countries, but there was no development of professionalization on the European and Latin American models, and consequently there was a failure to bring playing standards up to international level. But the game was popular everywhere, in the sense of being played and/or watched by considerable numbers of people, although it was a popularity which fluctuated with circumstance. We noted earlier that South Africa had three times played host to the Corinthians. All their matches were against white teams based on towns or provinces, with a few 'test' matches against South Africa thrown in. The Football Association sent a mixed amateur and professional team in 1910, which suggests an interest in furthering the game in an important part of the Empire, and standards were respectable. The Corinthians had lost five matches in 1907. Support was there too: 12,000 saw the Johannesburg Test of 1907, and 14,000 in 1910. The South African players had undertaken special training for the representative matches, and the FA's tour manager, perhaps over-charitably, claimed that the Test side played like an English First Division team and many of the town teams would have held their own in Division Two. Many of the players had learned the game in England and Scotland – three of the Corinthians who had toured in 1897 settled there – and by the eve of the First World War it looked to some contemporaries as though the game in South Africa was ready for its next step.

Indians and Africans, especially in Natal, had certainly been playing organized football before 1914. The Indians actually

sent a representative team to tour their home country at the
beginning of the 1920s, and welcomed a return visit in 1933. By
the inter-war years, every small town and mine had its football
club playing in league and cup competitions. Africans took up
the game in large numbers in the 1930s. Moreover, it continued to be popular among the white working class. Liverpool
in particular benefited from a steady stream of South African
footballers who came to join the English professional game.
But South African football was fragmented by race. There was
no overall administrative organization that could represent the
game as a whole and foster its development. Both the
Afrikaaner and English elite turned to Rugby Union, where
South Africa had already shown its ability to compete successfully with the British at one of their own games. Were it not for
racism and later the institutionalized 'separate development'
of apartheid, South Africa might by now have become the
most powerful football nation outside Europe and Latin
America.

   That Indian indentured labourers played football in South
Africa in the 1890s should alert us to the fact that, contrary to
much popular belief in the UK, the game was played in India
too, in Bombay and Delhi, but most notably in Bengal, and
overwhelmingly in Calcutta. The historian Percival Spear
emphasizes the way in which British games added another
string to India's cultural bow. India led the world in hockey,
but it was 'football in Bengal, tennis and cricket everywhere,
which have attained the level of addiction'. The game may
have been introduced in some of the schools as early as the
1880s and, as I have mentioned, football was an important part
of army life there. Christian high schools apparently played
against teams of British soldiers. Some indication of the
game's growing importance can be gauged by the notice taken,
even in the London *Times*, of the first defeat of a European
team by an Indian one, when Mohan Began beat the East
Yorkshire Regiment 2–1 in 1911. Eighty thousand people

were gathered in the Maidan in Calcutta. Most saw little of the game, but 'when it was known that the East Yorkshire Regiment had been beaten, the scene on the ground was astounding, the Bengalis tearing off their shirts and waving them. The absence of all racial feeling was noticeable.' Well perhaps not quite all. Bengali papers claimed that such a victory was proof of the physical potentialities of their race.

By the inter-war years there were at least three well-run divisions in the Calcutta Football League, with European teams, Anglo-Indian teams, Parsee teams, railway teams but also, most importantly, over 140 Indian teams in the city affiliated to the Indian FA (as against 14 European sides). Big crowds watched the matches and the Calcutta *Statesman* gave 'our chief hot weather amusement' as many column inches as it did to the game back home in Britain. At the end of each season, the Europeans played the Indians in an 'international match' and a crowd of 25,000, with many more locked outside, saw the Indians win 3–0 in 1929. No one reading the accounts of that match can doubt the importance of football in the local popular culture.

Why, then, had professionalism on the European model not come to Calcutta? The India FA was dominated by Europeans brought up to believe in the amateur tradition. Moreover, those values had been absorbed by the Indian middle class elite of lawyers, doctors and teachers and by the managers who ran the clubs and shared power with the Europeans on the Indian FA in the 1930s. There may well have existed Indian businessmen who would have been prepared to put up the money for a professional league in Calcutta, but they were effectively frozen out by the dominant values of the Raj. India was difficult terrain for the European football player, and did not attract the tours and coaches in the way that other countries did. But when the Islington Corinthians called in, on their 1937 world tour, they were astonished by the enthusiasm and commitment of players and spectators alike. And the British burra sahibs whispered in the ears of the Corinthians: 'You will win, won't you? Life will not be worth living if you don't.'

If football was popular in both India and South Africa, albeit not reaching the standards of Europe and Latin America, then we should not expect it to be lagging in another centre of British immigration and culture, Australia. And again, up to a point, we would be right. The Commonwealth of Australia boasted 1,200 football clubs by 1939, and all the states had football associations – ample testimony to the game's vigour. But an urban culture, and a largely British working-class emigration had not succeeded in making football Australia's national game, nor Australia a world football power.

The failure of the game to develop on a large scale in Melbourne is not perhaps too difficult to explain. Australian Rules got in first. This distant relation of Gaelic football was invented in the state of Victoria, and had its first set of rules drawn up in 1866, only three years after the Football Association in London had produced the first rules of Association Football and five years before the breakaway of the Rugby Union. The Victorian FA for the (Australian Rules) game was set up in 1877 and, most importantly, the game began to be taught in local schools. Some writers have argued that it was a more varied and interesting game than the earliest varieties of British football. It certainly showed that Victoria could break free of Britain's cultural grip. It filled a gap that might well have been plugged by football twenty years later.

But it did not spread to rival New South Wales. The fact that it was Victorian was probably enough to damn it. So why did British-style football not flourish around Sydney harbour? The answer in this case was the prevalence of Rugby Union and also, somewhat later, Rugby League. Soccer was again present but muted. The Corinthians never visited Australia and the FA toured there for the first time only in 1925. Rugby tours on the other hand followed hard on the early cricket visits. Perhaps, once more, it was a question of which game was supported by the most energetic members of the elite. The key decades would be the 1890s and 1900s, because it was in those years that rugby grew and soccer, relatively speaking, did not. Sydney could not have supported a league system based on all-out professionalism, but what was to prevent it from forming a part-time structure which could have raised standards closer to those of Europe?

If you ask why football failed to become the people's game in North America and most noticeably in the United States, then part of the answer would seem to be timing. The great trek from the old world to the new was largely over before 1914, in other words before football had really become the national game of so many European countries. Moreover, long before then America had had its own national game, baseball. This was a game allegedly all-American, invented there, perfected there and played to a standard no one else remotely approached. In millionaire sports goods entrepreneur Albert G. Spalding it had a propagandist who was second to none. It was also played in the summer, when football would also have to have been played. Even more crucially, by 1900, manifesting a knowledge of baseball was a relatively painless way for the immigrants to show commitment to their new country. Football, like communism, was an un-American activity.

Yet the early history of football in the United States would repay serious study. Like the British economy in the 1980s, the game there was always threatening to turn the corner but never quite managing to do it. Canada beat the United States in an international match in the same year, 1885, that saw professionalism legalized in England. Three years later, the Canadians sent a team, doubtless full of Scots, on a tour of the United Kingdom. A combined US/Canadian team repeated the visit in 1891–2. The Corinthians were told when they were there in 1906 that the game had taken root in the States and

was fast becoming a popular pastime. In 1907 the *Times* noted
with somewhat hypocritical satisfaction that, although up until
recently it had been the game of the British immigrant there
were now many teams without a single member, unlike in
Canada where the Anglo-Scots still dominated most elevens.
Football was certainly widespread in St Louis, among both
German and British migrants, and university students from
Princeton, Harvard and Philadelphia were dabbling in the
game when a British touring team arrived.

Efforts were made to stimulate growth from the east. Sir
Thomas Dewar, another Scot, donated a silver trophy for an
all-American cup. It was won by Brooklyn Field Club, and
later, more promisingly, by Bethlehem Steel and Fall River
Rovers. The United States sent a team to the 1924 Olympics
and actually reached the semi-final of the first World Cup.
Admittedly, it wasn't a vintage year, as only twelve countries
competed, but they did have 3–0 victories over Belgium and
Paraguay before meeting the Argentinians and the full array of
South American virtuosity. The Corinthians actually lost eight
matches out of twenty-two in Canada in 1924, but were
unbeaten in five games in America. One suspects that the
Corinthians were weaker than usual and came up against the
sharpness of the emigre Scots in Canada. In the States, on the
other hand, it was largely students and young graduates who
made up the teams, although they did meet professional sides
in Philadelphia and the Brooklyn Wanderers. But by 1930 college football had joined baseball on the platform of truly
American sports. Soccer, like cricket, was foreign and rele-
gated to consenting Anglophiles.

America established its own games, a new cultural world to
fit the new physical one. Both Australia and South Africa
found national satisfaction in taking on the British at rugby
and cricket and showing that long hours under a hot sun
developed rather than stunted manly qualities. Indian cricket
was eventually to do the same. To win at football for all those

three would perhaps have taken longer than in the still strictly
amateur world of Rugby Union. What the development of
football in these countries shows is that urbanization and local
community or ethnic rivalries are not enough to produce popularity and professionalism. The role of elites is vital. James
Walvin argues that the game flourished where Britain traded
but not where she exercised political control. But did we really
control South Africa after 1902? And football in India went
with a flourish, if not a professional one. Patterns of development are difficult to plot and even more difficult to explain. By
the time of the first World Cup in 1930, football was not quite
a world game but it came much closer to it than anything else.

How did Britain see the 1930 World Cup? The fact that no
British team went to the competition in 1930 and that Britain
had withdrawn from FIFA two years before suggests an ambivalence at best, and a haughty disdain at worst, for this world
game the British had done so much to nurture. Of course the
path of development had never been completely hazard-free.
Manchester United's visit to Budapest in 1908 had ended in
misunderstanding, with stones being thrown by an irate
crowd. The United management vowed never to go there
again. Two Sunderland players were sent off in Hamburg in
1913 for over-zealous attention to a German forward. When
Chelsea played Boca Juniors in Buenos Aires in 1929, one of
their players 'was struck a violent blow on the jaw by a spectator' and another, thinking he was about to be offered a handshake by one of the home players, received a severe kick
instead.

It *was* a different game abroad. Different conditions produced different styles and slight but irritating variations in the
interpretation of football's laws. The hard grounds of southern
Europe and South America caused high bounces and
demanded better ball control but they also induced high kick-
ing, which the British didn't like. The British shoulder charge
was outlawed everywhere except Britain, and the goalkeeper

abroad was offered excessive protection. In Argentina, referees rarely left the touchlines and were easily intimidated by crowds, who encroached on to the field on the flimsiest of pretexts. Even Corinthians were not always able to keep their upper lips stiff in the face of provocation. In Prague in 1909, a last minute penalty was awarded against them. After quite an argument, the alleged offender picked up the ball and glared defiance at the referee, who prudently blew for time. Pushing, elbowing and obstruction on one side was met by aggressive British tackling on the other. Worst of all, although many foreign players claimed to be amateurs, the British strongly suspected that they were not.

But there could be no argument that, after World War One, overseas players were much improved performers on the field. Uruguay surprised everyone by winning the football tournament at the 1924 Olympics. The president declared a national holiday, provided civil service jobs for the players, and issued a set of stamps. And they also won that first World Cup. Patronizing comments about 'futbol' in Spain were momentarily stifled when Spain became the first overseas team to defeat a full England side in Madrid in 1929. And after a summer's football-watching in Europe two years later, one English journalist ranked them only sixth best on the continent. Lacklustre performances by British professional clubs abroad led to suggestions from the Austrians, for example, that the teachers had nothing left to teach. It was about time for their pupils to offer them an education.

Note: This is not a subject on which much has been written but two fascinating and useful books are: Willy Meisl, *Soccer Revolution*, 1955 and R.B. Alway, *Football all Around the World*, 1948.

6. GOING GLOBAL: THE FIFA STORY

Alan Tomlinson

> The Prussians are a bunch of bastards . . . dirty square heads, mindless sheep without the slightest initiative and ready for the slaughter.
>
> > Henri Desgrange, founder of the Tour de France and sports paper editor, August 1914, quoted in Richard Holt, *Sport and Society in Modern France*, London: Macmillan 1981, p.195

> We must have the World Cup *because* we have nothing.
>
> > Carlos Ditterhorn, President of the Chilean Football Federation, on his country's successful candidature to host the 1962 Finals, made whilst earthquakes were shaking his country

Large-scale international sports were trapped, from their beginnings, in a major tension. They represented an attractive cosmopolitanism and a meeting ground between cultures. But equally they were always a forum for the assertion of particular national strengths. It was as if nations wanted to reach out to each other for a handshake whilst simultaneously puffing out their chests in pompous self-satisfaction. Nations struggling for a focused self-identity in their formative days were not slow to seize on sport as a potent weapon.

The game of football was exported to the world by all-confident Britons. Football became one of Britain's most successful cultural exports, more resoundingly successful than Shakespeare, and more smoothly adaptable than, say, a Gilbert and Sullivan opera. Football was exported as one of the means whereby allegedly uncivilized nations might be rendered civilized. The character-training bred in the public schools would fuel the ethos of the gentleman-amateur. Yet Britain, though offering the game to the world, did not then lead the internationalization of the game. As the game took a grip on the world, and as international matches assumed a tone of emphatic modernity – travel, tactics and the competitive element all packaged into assertive national formats – Britain stayed at home. The world governing body, FIFA (Fédération Internationale de Football Association) got off the ground with no initial help from the British and, particularly, with indifference bordering on contempt from the English footballing authority, the Football Association.

Recently FIFA celebrated its eightieth birthday with a self-confident ring of modernity. Hailing the achievements of its president, João Havelange, the organization chose to stress the direction FIFA has taken during his decade at the helm. With Havelange, FIFA has followed 'another direction, that of universality . . . the Brazilian president . . . applied methods in football which were long known in social, economic and political life' (*FIFA, 1904–1984*, p. 26). FIFA presents its current president as an uncompromising man of action, who offered a then-uncertain organization a 'necessary dynamism'. Look at any recent FIFA publication and you'll see a number of lucrative contract deals. On the back of a copy of *FIFA News* a few years ago: 'KLM, the "official FIFA airline"', salutes FIFA for its worldwide achievements in 'doing work for young people'. FIFA's self-image projects a cosmopolitan and confident universality. Its headquarters, nicely placed in neutral Switzerland, offers simultaneous translation, regular glossy communications for different interest groups within their worldwide constituency, and a sharp here-and-now image: 'The administration is managed in the form of a modern firm.'

FIFA, then, has successfully developed and kept an international dimension to football, whilst itself shifting with the times. From a small grouping of seven founder-member European associations in 1904, it has developed into a giant organization with 150 members and a dozen or so aspirant members jostling for top space on the waiting list.

How, then, did this achievement take place? And why was England, benevolent parent of the world game, sitting on the sidelines so often in the earlier days of FIFA story? The first years of FIFA were presided over by a French engineer/newspaper editor Robert Guérin; he was followed by D.B. Woolfalil, an English civil servant from Blackburn and integral contributor to Blackburn Rovers' domination of the English Cup in the 1880s; then the French lawyer Jules Rimet took over for several decades. FIFA today is in the hands of João Havelange, a suave Latin American lawyer/businessman. The pendulum of world footballing politics has swung dramatically towards the Third World.

FIFA started life in 1904. After seeking the unresponsive English association as leader and figurehead of the initiative, a group of seven European nations (Belgium, Denmark, France, the Netherlands, Spain, Sweden and Switzerland) founded the organization at a meeting in Paris. British associations, at the centre of the game's worldwide growth were conspicuously absent. The Frenchman Robert Guérin had suggested the formation of a European federation of nations to Frederick Wall, Secretary of the Football Association in England. Wall's response was that of the phlegmatic English upper class: 'The Council of the Football Association cannot see the advantages of such a Federation, but on all such matters upon which joint action was desirable they would be prepared to confer.'

Clearly Wall was suspicious to the point of an utter lack of

confidence concerning the competence of a group that he saw
as upstarts. For several years, the FA had deflected the
advances of its European neighbours. Belgium had
approached them at the end of the 1890s, in search of some
form of international collaboration. The Dutch had
approached the FA in 1902, suggesting the formation of an
international association which could focus upon the widespread European development of the game. Both these
approaches were left to languish within the bureaucratic procedures of an inefficient FA; it was as if to rush into action was
considered ungentlemanly.

Two decades after FIFA was formed, its first president,
Guérin, and the Dutchman Carl Hirschman said that they had
never been able to understand why the British gave no lead to
FIFA. Guérin recollected that after meeting Wall twice in 1903
he saw that for the moment at least he could get no further:
'Tiring of the struggle and recognizing that the Englishmen,
true to tradition, wanted to wait and watch, I undertook to
invite delegates from various nations myself.'

But as soon as FIFA looked strong enough to survive, the
English FA were ready to join the project. France had played
their first international match less than three weeks before the
meeting at which FIFA was formed. Denmark's first international was not to take place until the 1908 Olympics in London,
the year of Switzerland's first international matches. Spain
played its first international at the 1920 Olympic Games. So
FIFA's founding fathers were novices. Three of them (Sweden,
France and Spain) helped form FIFA before national Football
Associations had been formed in their own countries. In 1902,
in the first international match between non-British countries,
Austria beat Hungary 5–0. Other more experienced nations,
not just the British, were also notable by their absence from
the 1904 initiative.

It is not surprising, then, that the FA became more involved
through the proffering of advice and expertise. A special FA

committee asked Continental nations to a conference on the
eve of the 1905 England–Scotland match in London, after
which the British Associations accepted FIFA's general objectives and expressed a willingness to co-operate. The English FA
then soon decided that the only way to defend the game
against misinterpretations, and against intrusions into the
principles of amateurism, was to dominate it. This was
achieved by getting D.B. Woolfall, the Blackburn man,
elected as FIFA president. (Guérin had resigned after his efforts
to organize a first international competition came to nothing:
when his deadline for entries was reached, there were no
entrants.) This was how Woolfall summarized the attitude of
the FA after meeting with other nations in Berne in 1905:

> '. . . it is important to the FA and other European
> Associations that a properly constituted Federation should
> be established and the Football Association should use its
> influence to regulate football on the Continent as a pure
> sport and give all Continental Associations the full benefit
> of the many years' experience of the FA.'

The stress was on the 'proper' procedures, on the 'purity' of
the game, and on the importance of 'experience'.

Early attempts at a World Cup had foundered, and with
them the optimism of Robert Guérin. The Olympic Games
provided a form of official World Championship, but many of
the outstanding players of the era were denied participation by
their professional status. FIFA bumbled along quietly for a few
years, a growing, rather than a sleeping, giant, and then
started to consolidate its position in truly global terms after the
Great War.

Non-European members began to join before the War:
South Africa 1909-10; Argentina and Chile 1912; the USA
in 1913. Great Britain continued to take top honours in Euro-
pean-based Olympic tournaments, in 1900, 1908 and 1912.

After the Great War the face of world football began to change. In a controversial final in Antwerp in the 1920 Olympics, Belgium took the honours when, as they were leading 2–0, the Czech team walked off the pitch, claiming that dubious refereeing decisions were no accident! And in the 1924 Paris Olympics Final, Uruguay defeated Switzerland, evidence of the emerging strengths of the Latin American game.

This domination of the Olympic competition by the Uruguayan side helped provoke a long-standing controversy in the world game over the definition of the amateur. This controversy combined with political friction in Europe meant that the 1930s was a stormy but formative decade in the FIFA story. The England Association's main contribution to early world cups was to pretend that they did not matter.

The first World Cup in 1930 was the start of a period of sustained expansion. Figures on FIFA's growth, and on the scale of the World Cup itself, show clearly the truly global dimensions of this expansion:

Table 1: The Growth of FIFA

Year	Number of Associations
1904	7
1914	24
1920	20
1923	31
1930	41
1938	51
1950	73
1954	85
1959	95
1984	150

This has been a steady and even rate of growth in memberships with only one significant interruption – after the First World War. The balance of participation between different groupings of nations can be seen in Table 2.

In 1919, FIFA had wanted normal sporting relations restored, but delegates from the British Associations and from Belgium, Luxembourg, and France too, passed a resolution ostracizing the 'former enemy nations of Austria, Germany and Hungary'. A resolution was also passed ostracizing 'neutral associations' if they kept up playing contact with the defeated countries. This went too far for the neutral countries, who were unwilling to be dictated to in so complete a fashion. Denmark, Finland, Norway and Sweden expressed their intention to continue to keep up playing contacts with all countries. Italy expressed the same view. The boycotting group formed a new Federation of National Football Associations, and the English FA withdrew from FIFA. In 1920, Jules Rimet was made provisional head of FIFA. In 1921 he became official president, a post he was to hold for the next 33 years.

The new splinter group was a fragile body. Belgium and France soon had doubts about the proposal to boycott 'neutrals'. And within four years, helped by the need for British co-operation concerning Irish football in the newly partitioned Ireland, FIFA had persuaded the British Associations back into the fold, agreeing to the major prerequisites laid down by the British. One key point of tension remained: the definition of the amateur. It might seem odd that in a period of increasingly full-time commitment to a professionalizing game, British Associations should produce rifts in the international relations of sport by defending old notions of amateurism. Such defences have to be seen as a form of rearguard action, an attempt to impose traditional and established values on a situation fast getting out of control.

Having been wooed back into FIFA in the early 1920s, by 1928 the British again resigned. The 'amateur' issue had been a

Table 2: The World Cup Finals

Date	Winner	Venue	Attendances	Games	Teams	
1930	Uruguay	Uruguay	434,500	18	13	(8 Latin American, 4 European plus USA)
1934	Italy	Italy	395,000	17	16	(2 Latin American, 12 European plus USA and Egypt)
1938	Italy	France	483,000	18	15	(1 Latin American, 12 European plus Dutch East Indies, Cuba)
1950	Uruguay	Brazil	1,337,000	22	13	(6 Latin American, 6 European plus USA)
1954	West Germany	Switzerland	943,000	26	16	(3 Latin American, 11 European plus Turkey and Korea)
1958	Brazil	Sweden	868,000	35	16	(4 Latin American, 12 European)
1962	Brazil	Chile	776,000	32	16	(6 Latin American, 10 European)
1966	England	England	1,614,677	32	16	(5 Latin American, 10 European plus North Korea)

1970	Brazil	Mexico	1,673,975	32	16	(5 Latin American, 9 European plus Israel and Morocco)
1974	West Germany	West Germany	1,774,022	38	16	(4 Latin American, 9 European plus Australia, Zaire, Haiti)
1978	Argentina	Argentina	1,610,215	38	16	(4 Latin American, 10 European plus Tunisia and Iran)
1982	Italy	Spain	1,766,277	52	24	(6 Latin American, 14 European plus Cameroon, Kuwait, Algeria, New Zealand)
1986	?	Mexico	?	52	24	(5 Latin American, 14 European plus South Korea, Canada. Algeria, Morocco, Iraq)

threat to FIFA harmony, and when, in 1926, the International
Olympic Committee approved of 'broken time' payments for
competitors in the forthcoming Games, the old English dog
could no longer be held on its leash. The British response was
to reaffirm without any deviation whatsoever the British definition of amateur:

> Players are either amateur or professional. Any player
> registered with this Association as a professional or
> receiving remuneration or consideration of any sort above
> his necessary hotel and travelling expenses actually paid,
> shall be a professional. Training expenses of amateurs
> other than the wages paid to a trainer or coach must be paid
> by the players themselves. A player competing for any
> money prize in a football context shall be a professional.

This was pretty unambiguous stuff. Even professionals playing for their country were to experience this honest rigidity in
later years. Sir Stanley Matthews recollects his first game for
England against Wales at Cardiff a few weeks after the
appointment of Stanley Rous as FA Secretary:

> On the Saturday morning he got us all together to pay our
> fee and he had all these notes piled up on the desk and he
> paid us. I think we had £6 or £8. We had expenses . . . and
> we had little tickets and it said 'travelling', say from Stoke
> to Cardiff, 'afternoon tea' and you had to put your price in.
> You know in those days afternoon tea was 1/6d and if you
> overcharged . . . [the treasurer] already knew the prices
> and he'd say 'you've over-charged sixpence'.

Matthews also recollected the letters of selection internationals received, addressing them only by their surnames. It is
clear that the FA, though seeking to catch up with the modern
world, was still rooted in traditional relations of class privilege

and deference. This was the tension at the centre of the English FA's conflict with FIFA: it led to the withdrawal from FIFA in 1928.

The resolution to resign was passed unanimously by the delegates of the 'Associations of the United Kingdom'. The FA Conference Report stresses how the representatives of all four UK countries were convinced that 'they should be free to conduct their affairs the way their long experience has shown to be desirable'. The English FA was authorized to write to Carl Hirschmann; in its letter Britain's professional/amateur distinction was summarized, and the FIFA acceptance of 'broken time' payments criticized: the UK Associations 'are satisfied from their experience in years past that it will not work out satisfactorily'. Note, again, the paternal and patrician tone: 'The great majority of the Associations affiliated with La Fédération Internationale de Football Associations are of comparatively recent formation, and as a consequence cannot have the knowledge which only experience can bring.'

Resignation, then, but not total withdrawal. British teams continued to play internationals during these years of separatism. But they were not present at the birth of the World Cup. It took the trauma of modernization to bring the FA more truly into the fraught community of world football.

Nearly twenty years after their resignation, the British Associations rejoined. Rimet had built up good working relations with Rous, and the British celebrated their re-entry by hosting a Great Britain v FIFA match at Hampden Park, Scotland, at the end of the 1947 season. A 135,000 audience saw the British rout this world side 6–1. The receipts of £35,000 were gifted to FIFA.

Victorious from the war, triumphant on the pitch, magnanimous in their renewed membership, the British came out of self-imposed isolation very much on their own terms or so it seemed. The 1–0 defeat suffered by England at the hands of the USA in Brazil in 1950, England's first World Cup, was seen

as a dramatic aberration. The Hungarian rout of England in
1953 at Wembley was a confirmation, though, of the changing
balance of power in world football. This was also to be expressed in the shifting patterns of power between the nations,
especially in the emergence of the Third World countries
as equals, not just on the playing field, but also in the boardroom.

As the tournament has expanded in scale, goals have not
increased in number. Quite the reverse. The average number
of goals per game in the first tournaments was approximately
four. The highest ever number of goals per game was in the
1954 final – well over five. This fell to under four per game in
Brazil in 1958. In the five tournaments up to 1978 the figure
stayed below three.

But this should not lead us to contrast the present with a uto-
pian past. The World Cup has never been covered in, and so
bolstered by any mythology of idealism comparable to the
Olympic myth. World Cup history is riddled with examples of
open conflict and corruption. At the very first World Cup, the
journey proved too much for most European sides and the
hosts, Uruguay (Olympic champions in 1928 as well as 1924)
were so insulted by this that they stayed away from the next
two World Cups. On their own sub-continent, their 1930
World Cup triumph was not unanimously acclaimed. Disap-
pointed Argentina fans took Uruguay's victory in the final
rather badly, storming the Uruguayan Consulate in Buenos
Aires before being dispersed by gun-toting police. In 1934, the
finals were exploited unashamedly by Mussolini, who claimed
the 'azzurri' (the blues) for his own. Argentina refused to
travel to the 1938 finals in France, after having their own can-
didature as host-nations rejected. Mexico also withdrew, to be
replaced by Cuba. In 1950 in Brazil, only Yugoslavia, of the
Iron Curtain countries, made the trip. Germany was still, five
years after the end of the war, not accepted as a FIFA member.
Scotland felt unworthy of the honour of participation; coming

second in the British championship, a qualifying performance in the eyes of FIFA, was not a proud enough achievement for them. They had announced that they would compete only if they won the British championship. Argentina, with the competition on its own doorstep, did not even compete, after a disagreement with the Brazilian Federation. And France, generously invited (as FIFA and World Cup pioneers) to replace Turkey (another withdrawal) even though they had failed to qualify, themselves withdrew in a dispute over venues and travel schedules.

In the 1958 qualifying rounds, all Israel's opponents refused to play them. Wales, drawn out of a hat containing the names of other qualifying groups' runners-up, played off with the quarantined Israelis, beat them twice and went on to Scandinavian glory. Controversy reached hysterical heights in that tournament as the Swedes progressed further and further, and in their semi-final against the holders, West Germany, placed their own cheerleaders on the pitch to whip up the crowd, German cheerleaders being restricted to the running-track. They were forbidden from engaging in these extreme jingoistic practices for the Final against Brazil.

If a major source of early conflict between FIFA members was the question of amateurism, the issue of national status had also been central. As FIFA grew, these nationalist rivalries were as conflict-provoking as ever. They were also becoming re-defined in world terms. Alliances between blocs of Third World nations were the basis for the succession of João Havelange to the FIFA presidency. Between 1971 and 1973, Havelange visited 86 FIFA countries, concentrating his canvassing energies on Africa and Asia. Rous recalls how 'an Indian spoke against me and I was surprised at that. Countries like Indonesia voted against me . . . quite a few didn't really know me and they were persuaded to vote for Havelange.'

Havelange became FIFA's first non-European president. One of his campaigning commitments was to raise Third

World footballing standards generally. Coaching seminars, rather grandly framed as an International Academy, were organized, in Africa, Asia and Oceania. FIFA under Havelange introduced ambitious educational projects and a World Youth Championship (hosted by Tunisia, 1977; Japan, 1979; Australia, 1971; and Mexico, 1983); it also changed the rules of Olympic eligibility so that any European or South American player who had not participated in the previous World Cup could now play in the Olympics. Two developments under the influence of Havelange stand out: the expansion of the number of World Cup finalists, increased from the traditional 16 to 24 at the 1982 finals in Spain; and the introduction of sponsorship on a large scale. Under Havelange, FIFA strode into the modern world of sponsorship; Coca-Cola culture, one of the most advanced and sophisticated multinational strategies, provided the economic base for Havelange's ambitions. At the first World Cup to be played with expanded numbers, in Spain in 1982, an estimated £45 million was spent on preparing 17 stadia in 14 cities; and £15 million on hotels, roads and publicity (David Barnes, *World Cup, Spain 1982 – the game of the century*, London: Sidgwick & Jackson, 1982, p. 160). But the average attendance at games in Spain was the lowest since 1962 in Chile.

Parallels between Havelange's operations in Brazil and in the wider world are undeniable. An indiscriminately expanded Brazilian championship undermined the fabric of the game. Critics point out that this is precisely what is happening in the World Cup itself. In Brazil, the Brazilian Football Federation recognizes no difference between amateurs and professionals; there is no football league separate from the Football Association, as is the case in England. In the Brazilian Federation, each constituent unit has one vote. This means, to take an English analogy, that an amateur league club in Sussex would have the same voting power as Liverpool, Tottenham Hotspur or Manchester United. Control of the

Federation will go to those who divert resources to the poor and weak – buying their support, in effect. Havelange clearly learned his lesson well in his own country. A democracy based upon a premise of inequality of resources was a sound means of gaining unassailable power. Repeated effectively on the international scale, this has given Havelange *carte blanche* within FIFA. Opinion on the effects of Havelange's leadership has been divided. The English sports journalist Brian Glanville accuses him of having 'ruined the World Cup . . . sold it down the river to the Afro-Asians and their ilk', the European countries having 'truckled to the ineffable Havelange'. Granville's Eurocentric sneer fails to acknowledge some memorable and dramatic moments of World Cup History, which could not have happened had the best 16 teams in the world simply competed in the finals – Iran forcing their draw with Scotland in 1978; the North Koreans sending the Italians home on an early flight before losing in 1966; and the lively performances of Cameroon and New Zealand in 1982 – the role of the potential giant-killer has been a memorable one in recent World Cup competitions. To select finalists solely on the basis of merit would be to confirm the dominance of those countries where the best football is *now* played; it would do nothing to encourage the development of the game *worldwide*. Entries are now split into zones which include Africa, Asia/Oceania and Concacaf (Central and North America) as well as Europe and South America. Since his succession in 1974, Havelange has given FIFA a global presence.

The globalization that is at the centre of the FIFA story can only adequately be understood as one aspect of the shifting relations of international status, if not power. Sports, sporting achievements and sporting moments make massive contributions to the popular memory. In them, the re-presentation of history so central to the construction of national identity can be effectively achieved.

All nations, as Benedict Anderson has so eloquently argued

(*Imagined Communities – Reflections on the Origin and Spread of Nationalism*, London: Verso, 1983) have at some stage to indulge in some form of imagining. The nation, he suggests, is imagined on three levels: as limited, as having boundaries; as free, under the sovereign state; and as a community, 'conceived as deep, horizontal comradeship'. In this final level of imagining – that of the fraternal community – it is forms of symbolic action which state the case for the country itself. FIFA may have expressed, at various stages in its development, principles of world citizenship, or international understanding; but its major function has remained unchanged. It has offered, on the level of popular consciousness, a forum for the expression of different forms of national belonging and superiority. The history of FIFA reflects the fact that more and more countries are getting into the act of national self-definition.

I would like to thank David Barber, Press Officer of the (English) Football Association, John Humphrey, and Myrene Weller.

Details of World Cup history and incidents have been culled from two enormously useful sources which I have not cited directly in the chapter: Brian Glanville, *The History of the World Cup*, London: Faber & Faber, 1980; and Jack Rollins's *Complete World Cup Guide*, London: Sphere Books, 1982.

7. AND THE BONNIE SCOTLAND WILL BE THERE: FOOTBALL IN SCOTTISH CULTURE

Stuart Cosgrove

Sure it's a grand old team to play for,
And it's a grand old team to see.
And if you know your history,
It's enough to make your heart go OH OH OH OH!
We don't care what the English say,
What the hell do we care?
For we only know there's gonnae be a show
And the Bonnie Scotland will be there.'

To support Scotland is to invade the entire field of history. More than any other nation, including Brazil, the Scots elevate football to its proper status. In the words of the late Bill Shankly, the Scottish legend who managed Liverpool through the early years of their European triumphs, 'football is not a matter of life and death, it's far more important than that'. Football is simply the most significant national activity in Scotland. On the street corners, on television, at Hampden Park but most importantly on the bi-annual trips down to Wembley, football is the respirator. If you are male and working-class in Scotland and have no interest in football, then your life is simply a matter of slow suffocation, because football is the air we breathe.

The Scottish national experience finds its richest and most complex expression in football. The support for the national team is intensely patriotic, a reflection of the distinct sense of nationalism to be found in the character of most Scots. The

steady southward drift of professional footballers who leave
the poorer Scottish League to play for teams in the more lucrative English first division is a direct reflection of Scotland's historic migrancy – the emigration of young, often
unemployed, Scots, to find improved social conditions in England, Canada, Australia, New Zealand and the USA. The
much publicized rivalry between the Glasgow-based clubs Celtic and Rangers reflects the religious separatism which still
persists in Scottish education. It helps to confuse Scotland's
already tangled historical links with Ireland, continues to highlight the denominational difference between the protestant
majority and the catholic minority, and therefore acts as an
extension of freemasonry, the local system of business
interests which can often impede the employment and promotion prospects of catholic workers. The leaking stand roof at
Hampden Park and the plastic dustbins which double as toilets
outside the ground are an obvious manifestation of the material poverty of Scottish League football and hint at the
economic deprivation throughout many parts of the country.

The most obvious barometer of Scottish football is its support, and the least reliable is the drunken image of the 'typical'
Scotland fan, so beloved by Fleet Street. Scotland's supporters
are unquestionably partisan (and frequently drunk) but they
are also one of the most complicated groups of sports fans in
the world. Capable of rampant celebration and maudlin
lament, the fans are motivated by a dream, a dream that is
past, present and future, a dream that is always extended by
alcohol, and a dream that directly relates to the nation and its
progress. The dream is one of Denis Law's bicycle kicks, it's
Slim Jim Baxter making the ball talk, it's pulling on a navy jersey and it's King Kenny scoring through the English keeper's
legs. The dream is available every time Scotland play, but so
are the nightmares.

Scotland are a notoriously inconsistent football team, capable of substantial achievements and inconceivable disasters.

The team often has difficulty in overcoming vastly inferi or
opposition, but can retrieve that shortcoming by outclassing a
team having greater financial resources and a superior reputation. It was Scotland, living out the dream, who defeated England soon after their victory in the 1966 World Cup final, and it
was Scotland who travelled to Argentina, supremely confident
that only Brazil stood between them and the trophy, only to
stumble at the first hurdle by losing to Peru and then failing to
beat an unfancied Iranian side.

No other team torments its fans quite like Scotland. When
Hampden chants 'EASY' the team invariably punishes them by
making it difficult, but beneath the self-inflicted torture is an
impressive footballing history. For a small, under-resourced
country, Scotland produces a vast reservoir of footballing
talent which not only sustains the success of Scottish League
clubs, but partly sustains the success of the major English
clubs, and adds an aggressive dimension to teams in Italy and
elsewhere. In qualifying for every World Cup final since 1974,
the national team's achievements are only modest when seen
through the eyes of their own supporters, a tartan army which
believes with supreme optimism that Scotland should be able
to 'cuff' anyone who dares to play them. It is a belief fuelled by
arrogant chauvinism, but it is allowed to persist, simply
because the country continues to produce a wealth of so called
'tanner ba' players' who can delight crowds, and who, in the
case of former captain Archie Gemmill in the 1978 finals, can
dismantle a packed defence, score the tournament's best goal,
and conjure victory out of skill, conviction and necessity.

The 'tanner ba' player' is usually small, often ginger-haired,
invariably working-class and aggressively Scottish. In the past
it was Alan Morton, 'the wee Blue Devil', Billy Liddell, Wee
Willie Henderson, 'Jinky' Jimmy Johnstone, Billy Bremner
and Archie Gemmill; in the present it is Gordon Strachan, the
diminutive redhead who currently plays for Manchester

United. Like the Scotland team, the 'tanner ba' player' is inconsistent. Having learnt the game on waste ground and in backyards, practising daily with a 'tanner ba', a tennis ball or a punctured plastic Frido, he is capable of superb ball control and inspired skills. But on match day, the skills can be trapped by frustrating inactivity and bouts of uncharacteristic quietness. This inconsistency, or rather this capacity for opposing patterns of behaviour, lies at the heart of Scottish football. The reality of Scotland at play is the reality of a national schizophrenia, a split in the social personality, which reveals itself through competing public images. Scotland exists through opposites, a set of tensions between arrogance and modesty, material poverty and footballing wealth, national pride and public shame; the reality of being a small dependent country set against the desire to be independent and of monumental importance; and finally the irresolvable dialectic between getting drunk and sobering up. These are Scotland's perpetual headaches: the hangover of football elevated to national culture.

Scotland's national predicament is always seen in relation to England, the nation that has historically suppressed Scottish interests. It was the Irish writer Brendan Behan who identified the problem:'God help the poor Scots; they'll never be free but we're entirely surrounded by water.' Scotland's relationship with England lies at the centre of our national schizophrenia, a tension between dependence and independence which inevitably spills over into football. The song says 'We don't care what the English say' but the fans know it's their form of camouflage. Of course we care. When the TV commentator Jimmy Hill described a Scotland goal against Brazil as a 'toe-poke', BBC switchboards were jammed within minutes. When the evening news is broadcast, it regularly announces new redundancy schemes at Ravenscraig and Gartcosh. From Jimmy Hill to Margaret Thatcher, Scotland spends most of its time *having* to listen to England.

Alongside Scotland's sense of dependence and independence is an attitude to drink. To understand Scotland, you
have to know the tension between drunkenness and sobriety
and the distinctions between those who drink too much and
those who never touch a drop. On the one hand there is the
noisy and demonstrative image of the tartan army, decked in
flags and tearing up the turf; on the other, looking on in quiet
and tolerant disbelief, is the humourless face of a thousand
dour Scots. As the renegades rip up the pitch, the rational side
of Scotland's social personality stands aside; two attitudes
united by their patriotism. This essay centres on the most significant of those tensions, the struggle between the renegades
and the rationalists, and between two mythical footballing
figures, Willie Johnston and Jock Stein.

Willie Johnston is the epitome of the wayward side of Scotland's social personality. A winger of outstanding skill, fast
enough to compete at the highest athletic level and a cavalier
'tanner ba' player', he was guaranteed to excite crowds.
Johnston was the ultimate renegade, known universally as the
player sent home in disgrace from Argentina for taking pro-
scribed drugs, he was eventually banned from playing for Scotland for life. Sent off more than any other Scottish interna
tional in football history, Johnston had a short and passionate
temper. His emotional commitment was beyond question. He
was simply a Scots fan on the wing. Even now, years after he
ceased to play for Scotland, Johnston, or 'Wee Bud' as he is
warmly known, is still a legendary figure. His anti-authorita-
rian behaviour both on and off the pitch make him a perfect
character in the mythology of renegade Scotland. As a club
player, he once picked up a can thrown from the terraces and
interrupted the flow of the game in order to drink the can's
unknown contents. Bud has bared his arse to referees, managers and players alike, and, if myth is to be believed, he once
lived out the Scots fan's ultimate dream: sitting on the ball as
he beckoned to the English defence in a mixed gesture of arro-

gance, superiority and supreme ball-control.

Johnston is from the mining districts of Fife, one of the most important breeding grounds of Scottish professional football. His career at Rangers and later at Heart of Midlothian places him firmly as a player with a protestant identity, whilst his reverse mirror image, Big Joe Jordan, the toothless striker, is a catholic. Separated by religion, Johnston and Jordan are united by their renegade behaviour and by their close affinity with the Scottish support. Jordan is famous for his aggression and for a controversial incident in the qualifying stages of the 1978 World Cup, when he clearly handled the ball in the box then duped the referee into awarding Scotland a penalty. Although he still persists in declaring his innocence, television highlights appear to show Jordan kissing his hand and gesturing in secret to the Scotland fans. The image is unambiguous – 'Look I'm one of you, I'd lie through my teeth for Scotland' – the very teeth he leaves in his jacket pocket before each game, not only to enhance his hard-man image but, as the joke goes, to protect his wallet in case Willie Johnston is sent off early and decides to raid the pockets. Scots fans love to perpetuate a criminal self-image; it is a sure sign of their renegade reputation. The same sort of joking self-denigration is celebrated in the song 'We're the worst-behaved supporters in the land', a popular chant in the 1970s, when the English media regularly ran features on the 'hooligan excesses' of the tartan army.

Alongside Johnston and Jordan in the folklore of renegade patriotism are the Copenhagen Five, a group of Scottish players, including the captain Billy Bremner, who were banned by the Scottish Football Association after a much publicized bender in Denmark when team members and fans fought with bouncers and the local police in a nightclub. The press were not slow to draw parallels between the behaviour of the players and the antics of the most unruly elements within the tartan army. And the hustlers were not slow to cash in. Blackpool stall-holders prepared for the annual Glasgow Fair

fortnight by selling joke banknotes called 'Copenhagen Fivers'
which replaced the Queen's head with the faces of the five
accused.

The most triumphant and ultimately tragic period of Scotland's renegade patriotism coincided with Allie McLeod's
infamous reign as manager, in the period leading to Scotland's
involvement in the 1978 World Cup finals in Argentina.
McLeod's managerial style was flamboyant, noisy, undiscip-
lined and fiercely partisan; at last one of the tartan army had
made it to the manager's chair. He allowed the team to live a
public and excessive social life prior to their departure for
Argentina. This included a reported fight at the team's hotel in
Dunblane and a less publicized incident in which prominent
players joined fans as they urinated up a close next to the
Shanghai chip-shop in Perth. On the following day, Scotland,
with several sore heads in their midst, defeated England and
the incident was forgotten.

The Argentina campaign brought to a head a sustained
period of Scottish nationalism which had grown in momentum
throughout the 1970s. For long periods over the preceding
twelve years, the Scottish National Party (SNP) were the fastest
growing political party in Europe, and they competed for the
nationalist vote with a newly formed political party, the Scottish Labour Party (SLP), an organization which combined
nationalism with working-class labourism. The rise of Scottish
nationalism in the 1970s was undoubtedly linked to the con-
troversies surrounding North Sea Oil, which the SNP, with considerable justification, claimed was not being used to the
economic advantage of Scotland and its people. The sight of
oil resources disappearing to the advantage of American,
Dutch and English corporations coincided with the radical
decline of Scotland's heavy industries, particularly steel, coal
and shipbuilding. The rise in importance of a strip through
central Scotland known as 'Silicon Glen', which took its name
from the proliferation of computer-based light industries,

merely complicated the worries. As Scotland's economic
wealth was either in deep decline or disappearing overseas, the
country was becoming a new site for cheap labour, a convenient outpost for the hi-tech multinationals of America and
Japan.

Scotland's increased awareness of economic exploitation
and the resultant upsurge in political nationalism inevitably
spilled over into football. The name 'tartan army' – the collective term used by media and fans alike to describe Scotland's
flamboyant supporters – was consciously adopted from the
name of a militant nationalist faction which advocated
paramilitary action, successfully blew up oil-pipelines and was
involved in a bungled bank robbery in Glasgow. The cultural-
nationalist group 'Seed Of The Gael' regularly handed out
political leaflets at Scotland games, and the song which eventually became the tartan army's favourite anthem began as a
folk song specially written for the nationalist movement. 'Oh
Flower Of Scotland', written and performed by The Corries,
encapsulated a popular sense of Scottish pride and independence, and instantly spread from folk clubs to hogmanay parties and finally to the terraces at Hampden.

'Oh Flower Of Scotland' mourns the historic defeat at Cul-
loden and laments the massacre of a whole generation of
young Scots (the flower of Scotland). But the chorus turns
from lament to triumph and acts as a positive declaration of the
youth of Scotland's commitment to independence and the dis-
bandment of the union with Britain.

> Those days are gone now and in the past they must remain,
> But we can still rise now and be a nation again.
> And stand against them, proud Edward's army,
> And send them homewards to think again.

The loudest chorus of 'Oh Flower Of Scotland' and the most
public demonstration of Scottish patriotism took place in Lon-

don over a famous weekend in 1977. By accident rather than design, the annual Scotland v England fixture fell on the same weekend as the Queen's Silver Jubilee. London and the south-east of England were decked out in royalist bunting; red, blue and white streamed overhead, and every second window was decorated with images of the royal family. From the Thursday morning onwards, Scots fans began arriving at Euston and Kings Cross carrying bags, banners, tartan regalia and enough liquid to drown London. By Saturday morning, an estimated 80,000 Scots fans, flying the lion rampant, a flag which by ancient statute is still illegal under English law, were celebrating on the streets and in the fountains of the West End. For three days, the Scots supporters had been setting fire to Jubilee bunting and replacing the Union Jack with Scotland's national flag, the St Andrew's Cross. When Scotland lived out the dream and won the game, Wembley Stadium witnessed scenes of incomparable celebration. Thousands of Scots fans – young and old, male and female – invaded the pitch, tore up the turf and carried the goalposts home to Scotland. The English press treated the invasion in the only way they knew how – 'Tartan Terror' – drawing on the now commonplace themes of football violence, drunkenness and criminality. The tartan army had a different explanation. Thousands returned home in buses, on special trains and by car, singing their new anthem: 'Gie Us An Assembly and We'll Gie Ye Back Yir Wembley'. The assembly never materialized, so the turf still grows in the back gardens of Kilmarnock and Kinross.

If Willie Johnston, Joe Jordan, the Copenhagen Five and the stolen pitch are lasting images of Scotland's renegade patriotism, then the late Jock Stein, Scotland's manager until his tragic death on 10 September 1985, is the other side of the social personality. Stein's attitudes and his managerial style were marked by a pragmatic, rational and sometimes dour public profile. He refused to be over-confident and often acted as a sobering corrective to the tartan army's more demonstrative activities. Jock Stein was an authoritative figure, possibly the most important personality in the history of Scottish football, and during his period as manager he presided over a quiet yet effective purge. To be sent off in a Scotland jersey (as in the case of the attacking full-back Ray Stewart) meant an early end to your international career; misbehaviour was seen as a disgrace, no longer an inverted triumph. Stein even tried the impossible, attempting to convince Scots fans that the annual game against England was of little significance when set next to a World Cup or European qualifying tie. He never quite achieved the impossible, perhaps because he never fully believed it himself: the powerful sway of patriotism was always there, suppressed beneath Stein's rationalism.

Jock Stein acted as a link figure in Scottish football. He shared the Irish boxer Barry McGuigan's ability to bridge denominational gaps. A protestant miner who went on to manage the 'catholic' Celtic to their greatest victory in the European Cup Final in 1967, he helped reduce the sectarianism in Scottish League football. Players were bought and sold on merit alone; he insisted that the Irish republican tricolour flag which flew provocatively over Celtic Park should be replaced with the League flag; and he regularly selected Scottish sides which refused to pander to the sectarian interests of either Celtic or Rangers diehards. If Stein showed bias it was to labourism – the old but powerful image that Scotland, its people and their football, was a communion of all that is positive about working-class culture. Along with Matt Busby of Manchester United and Bill Shankly of Liverpool, Stein was the ordinary coalminer who took the values of pit-face commonsense and applied them to football.

Stein's period of management coincided with two significant social campaigns in the wider arena of civic politics and national health-care. The campaign entitled 'Glasgow's Miles Better', a worldwide effort to improve Glasgow's negative and violent image, was a public relations exercise which accompanied a massive civic commitment to improve housing and social conditions. Meanwhile, the Scottish Health Council embarked on a major campaign to combat Scotland's poor health record. In 1977 the statistics on personal health demonstrated that 5,000 Scots died every year as a result of smoking; that Scots had the worst teeth in Europe; that 22,000 Scots died every year as a result of heart disease, often brought on by drink and cigarettes; and that Scotland had the highest rate of lung cancer in the world. The Scottish Health Council's Education Group promoted a high-profile campaign which included posters, cartoons and television advertising. Throughout the campaign, the viewer was hailed as a Scottish football fan: 'Here's tae us, wha's like us? Are we really "the people"? When it comes to ill-health, we the Scots are the champions.'

The campaigns on housing and health ran directly counter to the tartan army's self-image as the hardest fighting, heaviest drinking and most anti-social fans in the world. Sport was always supposed to be about fitness and health but for many Scots, football was a way of glorifying ill-health. The posters refused to accept this negative image and refused to pull punches: 'Visit your dentist regularly (and that means more regularly than Scotland wins the World Cup).' The cartoons dealt in hard-hitting home truths. As a drunk props up the bar, nearby football fans wonder if he'll make the game: 'He's no sportin' his colours. Apart fae the purple nose, red eyes and yellow fingers.' The television adverts were blunt condemnations of excessive drinking. An alcoholic fan does the unimaginable and sells his ticket in order to buy more drink. His friends leave for the game in disgust: 'we'll no support him anymore', they agree, in a play on the words of the tartan army song 'Bonnie Scotland We'll Support You Evermore'.

The fact that Stein's period as manager of the national side roughly coincided with the campaigns to change the image of Glasgow and its citizens is, in retrospect, highly significant.

The Stein regime was equally concerned with material change and redefining the public's image of Scotland. From 1978 to the present day he attempted, with some success, to secure consistency, but more importantly he transformed the team's public profile and improved the accountability of the players and their fans. Stein's 'social responsibility' was in some ways a conscious reaction against the renegade patriotism of the previous years and a rejection of the noisy and partisan style of the previous manager Ally McLeod.

Scotland has always engaged in a dialogue between nationalism and welfare socialism. When the rest of Britain swung towards the Conservatives at the last election, Scotland redistributed its nationalist vote and confounded electoral trends elsewhere by swinging in favour of the Labour Party. The Conservative option and the fiercely English image of its leader Margaret Thatcher was patently unattractive to most working-class Scots. Stein was typically cautious about how he cast his vote, but his closest friends and colleagues seemed to see politics and social responsibility in the way he managed football players. Bill Shankly once described Stein as the 'Scot who put socialism into action', and the former Celtic captain Billy McNeill described him as someone who 'intrinsically understood the working class'. The tragedy of his death (he died while watching Scotland play) was sharpened by his close knowledge of the Scottish working class, the desire to see their greatest dream lived out as reality.

Unlike his predecessor Ally McLeod, Stein chose a route governed by rationalism. He refused to allow his patriotic heart to rule his managerial head and he preached the careful philosophy that to win modestly was better than putting on a show. As if putting socialism into action, he dismantled the star system. No player was singled out for special praise; no one was bigger than the collective effort of the Scottish team; no one was too important to drop; and, in a thinly disguised punishment, 'Champagne' Charlie Nicholas sat on the substitutes' bench, a public reminder that the world of nightclubs, extravagance and media hype had no place in Stein's team.

Jock Stein knew Scotland, its fans and their national history better than any essay can explain. He knew that what they wanted was there for the taking, yet somehow out of their reach. He died of a heart attack knowing that a draw against Wales was enough to secure Scotland's progress in the World Cup, and knowing that the dream was on again. Scotland's goal, scored almost inevitably by a 'tanner ba' player' (the Rangers' winger Davie Cooper), was the final excitement which led directly to his death. The tartan army went into over-drive and greeted the result with their renegade anthem 'We're Gonnae Celebrate', but as the news of Stein's death spread round the ground the celebration turned to disbelief, then realization, and finally public grief. It was probably Scot-land's saddest and finest footballing moment, because it was uniquely Scottish, a national culture frozen into the opposed emotions of celebration and lament.

Whether the legacy of Stein's rationalism leads Scotland to success in Mexico or whether the players, goaded on by their loyal tartan army, press another self-destruct button, remains to be seen. Some will stay sober, most will get drunk. But which side of Scotland's social personality will triumph? Like the dream on which it's based, that remains beyond our knowl-edge. For we only know that there's gonnae be a show. And the Bonnie Scotland will be there.

With special thanks to Mike, Stuart, Rab, Geordie, Beggar and Tequila Tam, the man who fell to Perth.

8. 1966 AND ALL THAT: ENGLAND'S WORLD CUP VICTORY

John Clarke and Chas Critcher

It is said that most people can remember where they were and what they were doing when told of the death of President Kennedy. As memorable, is the day England's team won the World Cup in July 1966. We remember the event (appropriately, since for most people it was relayed by television) as a series of images: Ramsey's dignified walk across the turf at the end of ninety minutes; Hurst's shot bouncing ambiguously over – or was it only on? – the line; Stiles doing a jig at the end. Perhaps, too, we recall the words of commentator Kenneth Wolstenholme as Hurst moved in to score England's final goal: 'Some people are on the pitch, they think it's all over . . . it is now!' Even those for whom this is a received memory will know most of the English team: Banks, Cohen, Wilson, Stiles, Charlton, Moore, Ball, Hunt, Charlton, Hurst, Peters.

Only two other moments in the previous twenty-five years had assumed such symbolic importance for the English. One had been the national celebration of VE day in 1945; the other was the year of 1953, marked by the coronation of an English queen, an Englishman being one of the first to conquer Mount Everest and, for football followers at least, the Stanley Matthews Cup Final. But, just as the humiliation of the 1956 Suez Crisis was a counterpoint to the patriotism of 1953, in its revelation of Britain's loss of status as a world power, so, in football, the assumption of English superiority was being undermined even as it was being reaffirmed. The national side of Hungary, current Olympic champions, became the first

foreign side to beat England at Wembley. Their 6–3 victory
was confirmed by an even greater margin of 7–1 in the return
match. The 1966 victory seemed to show that the intervening
thirteen years had not been wasted. If we were going to have to
join the Common Market, at least we were undeniably self-
sufficient in football.

The connections between football, its cultural processes and
symbolic moments, and the national sense of England as a
political, economic and social entity, seem especially close in
the 1950s and 1960s. In this article we are concerned with how
1966 was, or could be taken to represent, not merely a moment
of footballing history, but a moment in the history of English
culture as a whole. First, though, we deal with what the World
Cup victory of 1966 appeared to mean for English football.

In retrospect, the 1966 World Cup marks a turning-point in
the history of the game in England: the advent of modern football. On the other side of this watershed lies the scarcely recog-
nizable football of the 1940s and 1950s. Massive and mostly
well-behaved crowds flocked to watch footballers, paid a
'fixed' maximum (and minimal) wage, play with an absorbent
leather football in ill-fitting, longsleeved shirts, baggy shorts
and leather-soled, nail-studded boots. Matches were played
without benefit of floodlights, substitutes or sponsorship.
Teams were picked, appeared in programmes, and played, in a
W/M formation unchanged since the early '30s.

Many of these features of English football changed indepen-
dently of the World Cup. Players' wages and contracts became
less feudal following the abolition of the maximum wage in
1961 and George Eastham's successful court case against Newcastle United two years later. (The winning World Cup team
shared £28,000 out of a total competition profit of a million
pounds). Crowds had slowly but significantly started to fall in
the early 1960s, as alternatives were provided by an 'affluent'
consumer society whose growing fashion-consciousness was
reflected in the more streamlined kit of footballers. The style

of play, however, remained unaffected by the economics of affluence. Clubs and national sides still fielded a goalkeeper, two full-backs, a centre-half (effectively a third back), two wing-halves, two inside-forwards, a centre-forward and two wingers.

Just as the economy responded sluggishly and reluctantly to the need to compete in changing international conditions, so did English football stick to established methods. Traditional means were still tried even when they could no longer be trusted. The illusion of England's international footballing supremacy – sustained in the inter-war period by self-exclusion from the World Cup, a politically motivated (and unrepresentative) selection of opponents, and a genuine invincibility at home – had been shattered by the Hungarian victories. More discerning commentators realized that England had fallen behind other nations and something would have to be done.

Little was. Walter Winterbottom, head of FA coaching and part-time England manager, fretted at the restrictions of selection by committee, the paucity of team practice sessions and the sheer mundaneness of English league football. In the 1950 World Cup finals, England had lost 0–1 to the USA and had subsequently been eliminated from their group by Spain. In 1954, they lost 2–4 in the quarter-finals to Uruguay. After the youthful promise of a national side built around Manchester United players had been destroyed by the Munich air disaster, England was eliminated from the 1958 World Cup by the USSR in a group play off. In 1962, England won only one match and were knocked out in the quarter-finals by Brazil. In four World Cups, England had played 14 matches, won 3, drawn 9 and lost 6, scoring 19 goals and conceding 21. Winterbottom was disillusioned and resigned, and was replaced as full-time manager by Alf Ramsey. An outstanding full-back for Spurs and England (who played in both Hungarian defeats, typically blaming the first on England defensive lapses), Ramsey had taken Ipswich to the league title in 1961–2. He had fashioned an all-conquering side from limited individual resources, often able to outwit opponents by tactical foresight and teamwork.

His first match as England manager brought a 5–2 defeat in Paris in 1962, which eliminated England from the European Championship. Three and a half years later England were world champions. Not only the substance but the manner of this achievement was to ensure as much continuity as change in the tactical evolution of English football.

Ramsey's great local success with Ipswich and international success with England was to leave a legacy of caution and dullness in the English game. His initial priority was to ensure defensive adequacy, at the expense, if necessary, of attacking abilities. As the results in the years between the France defeat and the onset of the World Cup showed, this he gradually achieved:

England v National Sides

	P	W	D	L	F	A
1963–4	13	7	4	2	39	20
1965–6	13	10	2	1	25	7

By the time of the World Cup, England's defence was settled and remained so for its duration. The evidence does not bear out the charge that Ramsey never had time for exceptional players or wingers. Greaves played in all three qualifying matches, as did a winger, even if their rapid succession – Connelly, Paine, Callaghan – demonstrated Ramsey's dissatisfaction with their individual quality. In the quarter-finals, Hurst was brought in for Greaves, and Ball was reinstated in place of a winger. The resulting formation was essentially 4-4-2, though the licence given to Charlton and Peters to roam behind Hurst and Hunt made it more flexible than its subsequent replicas would be.

England's victory in 1966 was the high point of a number of

triumphs by British clubs. Tottenham won the European Cup
Winners Cup in 1962–3 as did West Ham in 1964-5; Celtic won
the European Cup in 1967 followed by Manchester United in
1968; English clubs won the European Fairs Cup on four consecutive occasions between 1968 and 1971. The ghosts of the
'magical Magyars' had finally been exorcised:

> By the mid-1960s British football, having borrowed
> hungrily from other countries' methods and even
> character, and at last having adapted to its own tradition
> and temperament, was recognized as a major international
> force again.
>   (A. Hopcraft, *The Football Man*, Harmondsworth:
>   Penguin, 1971, p. 186)

The problem, for assessing the revival of British football,
was to weigh the factors contributing to it. For some, including
Ramsey himself, what was significant – and what needed to
continue – was The System, rather than the process of innovation:

> His uncompromising functionalism won a World Cup and
> set a trend that was copied throughout our national game.
> Since then Ramsey has been a prisoner of his own success,
> the emphasis on sweat and versatility inimical to the
> development of gifted individualism. He can only select as
> he finds and it is the hard and the fast who abound in
> English football.
>   (T. Pawson, *The Football Managers*, London:
>   Eyre-Methuen, 1973, p. 51)

The effects of Ramsey's solution and its imitation by less
gifted managers were considerable. In the years immediately
after the World Cup the annual total of English league goals
declined from six to five thousand. This goal-famine ended the

return to First Division grounds of the spectators who had
drifted away in the early 1960s. By 1970 Arsenal and Leeds
were the dominant sides, and gates had reverted to their pre-
'66 levels. Don Revie's often brilliant but frequently over-
cautious methods stressed work-rate as much as flair, contain-
ment as much as adventure, and the system more than the individual star. And Bertie Mee's Arsenal won the League and
Cup double with a team recollected in the popular memory of
the game as functional rather than dazzling, with hard-work-
ing ball-winners at the heart of the team.

Such club-based successes were soon exposed as an
inadequate basis for international achievement. Despite the
continued and remarkable record of club successes in Europe,
during which individual deficiencies were compensated for
through exceptional team work and an extensive use of Scottish, Welsh and Irish players, the English national side was
once again in a state of crisis. Failures to qualify for either the
1974 or the 1978 World Cup finals, were hardly alleviated by a
modest showing in 1982. (Even during the relatively successful
performances in the qualifying competition for 1986, two goal-
less home draws against Rumania and Northern Ireland were a
reminder of old failings. The inability to know what to do with
the ball when in possession was as prevalent as ever.)

The achievements of 1966, and the methods which produced
it, had failed to guarantee lasting success. The problem, which
1966 disguised, was that the English *cultural* tradition, based
above all else on a particular conception of manliness, had not
been revolutionized. The very pragmatism of Ramscy's
strategy was less his own than typical of the general tradition.
The English solution to the problems posed by European and
South American teams was not to increase the range and depth
of technical skill but to rely on existing strengths. Hence the
essence of the English approach was and still is to believe that
tactical planning and determination can be made to overcome
greater technical skill.

A book published even as the World Cup was taking place identified the problem. It was not the sort of system adopted by English football which was at fault, but its very obsession with system:

> A formation was seen and still is seen on the Continent as a bare framework for team positioning; it never or rarely hinders the individuality, creativeness and originality of a player. It is used merely as a mild form of discipline to give some order to the wanderings of ten players on the field. In England, however, partly because of our conservative nature and partly because we believed Arsenal's success was due entirely to the formation they used, namely the W/M, we have stuck too close to the theoretical positioning of players and their theoretical roles in a formation. Stereotyped play has resulted.
>
> (C. Lodziak, *Understanding Soccer Tactics*,
> London: Faber & Faber, 1966 p. 36

Twenty years later, the form has changed – W/M replaced successively by 4-2-4, 4-4-3 and 4-4-2, but the content remains the same. The real victor of 1966 was the deeply conservative and nationally characteristic instincts of English football, its preference for tall, heavy men at the back, strength in midfield and hardiness up front. This quintessentially English style of the World Cup winning team was also the style of its individual players. As components of a unit, they seemed to embody the corporate soul of English football: the uncanny anticipation of Banks, the coolness of Cohen and Wilson; the strong running of Hurst and Hunt, the elegance of Peters; the contrast between the immaculately groomed figure of Bobby Moore and the presence of Nobby Stiles – toothless grin, socks round ankles, snapping at the heels of opponents. Cutting less of a figure, but vital in the final, was Alan Ball:

When the old-time players and spectators say the game is not what it was, they are right. The application of new, elaborate and technical training programmes, and above all the tactical thought and planning preceding every season, every game, have pushed the emphasis further away from individual improvisation towards collective, integrated team work. This shift has inevitably promoted a new player . . . personified in Alan Ball . . . All the adjectives, the superlatives as well as the cliches which surround the modern player apply to Ball – the 90-minute man, genius clothed in sweat, perpetual motion, the essential team-man, hating to lose, living and breathing the game, awesome opponent and valued colleague, selfless yet still essentially a star . . . these are the terms in which one talks of Ball.

(David Miller in *Soccer Stars of Today*, ed. R. Hayter: Pelham, 1970, p. 42

If Ball stood for the future, the Charlton brothers embodied English manhood as it was known and recognized in the present:

Bobby and Jack played in all of England's World Cup matches; the two Charltons could be observed by the whole nation as brothers of vivid footballing character and self-portraiture – so dissimilar, yet each, in his own way expressing Englishness. Bobby graceful, cultured, creative, conveying some sort of artistic instinct: and, in the English tradition, a sense of restrained emotion, a faint air of diffidence overlying his talents and his endeavour. And Jack the honest artisan, straight as a gun barrel, stiff as a sentry, solid, stout-hearted, dependable. Foreigners must have seen it too.

(Norman Harris, *The Charlton Brothers*, London: Stanley Paul, 1971, p. 86

Thus the supremacy of England was confirmed not only by the fact but also by the manner and the bearers of victory. They had beaten the world, not by forsaking their English character but by exploiting key virtues to the utmost: discipline and organization, the sacrifice of individual needs to those of the team, a determination to overcome a better-equipped enemy. Echoes of World War Two, most visibly in the recurrent comparison of the victory celebrations with VE day, were not entirely inappropriate, for the team was seen to symbolize English virtues which had purchase outside a mere game. As the *Times* had noted a decade earlier: 'The ordinary man finds the form of our professional footballers a more convenient indication of the state of the nation than all the economist's soundings.' (The *Times*, 1 January 1955)

The *Times*'s observation on the relationship between the state of the game and the state of the nation is one which points to the intimate connection between sport and ideas of our national character. While the 1966 victory was a landmark in the footballing history of post-war England, it is also intimately linked with a wider set of images about British society and its development during the 1960s.

Our discussion of the 1966 World Cup win has so far focused mainly on the English national team. When we move to consider its relationship with the wider social and cultural environment, we are dealing with *British* society, and images of *British* character and cultural change. This change of 'national' emphasis is in some ways less striking than it appears. Within the dominant ideas of Britain, and British character and culture, England and 'Englishness' have always been allocated the leading role. Economically, politically and culturally, the other nations have been subordinated to England.

Sport is a central part of how we have come to see ourselves as a nation. Because of that, the fortunes of the national team, playing the national game, have acted as a very sensitive popular indicator of the state of the nation. The decline of the national team in the post-war era provided a telling reminder of the failing fortunes of a Britain losing not only its Empire, but also its imperial role and status. The loss of colonies, the 'granting' of independence, the fiasco of Suez seemed to be mirrored in our footballing failures. Somehow, it appeared that the traditional British virtues were no longer adequate. Lionhearted manliness appeared anachronistic. The question was: could Britain find a new role and a new national character and direction? It was posed, as a barometer of the nation's health, in the *Times* leader column:

> The fact is that in far too many fields the British seem to find it difficult to pursue excellence with the same intensity as other countries. This may make for more comfortable living, but there is no excuse for being unaware of the way in which other countries are forging ahead in the fields where Britain once led.
>
> (The *Times*, 23 September 1964)

This crisis of national identity seemed to have found its symbolic resolution in the 1966 victory. Yet even in the hour of national triumph, the divisions which lay beneath the surface of unity were apparent. This is nicely caught in Arthur Hopcraft's account of the competition. Genuinely national experiences were to be seen in the sense of carnival, the continuous focus of attention not only on the English team but also on the 'giant-killers' of North Korea, and the common delight at the final outcome. Football was, however, the expression of a distinctively class culture. The sudden interest in the World Cup of sections of the population normally indifferent to 'soccer' are evidence of a nationalism which incidentally happened upon football. Hopcraft's resentment against some of the occupants of the expensive seats at the World Cup final makes the point:

They were not football followers. They kept asking each
other about the identity of the English players . . . They
were there in their rugby club blazers, with their Home
Counties accents and obsolete prejudices, to see the
successors of the Battle of Britain pilots whack the Hun
again. Some of them wept a bit at the end and they sang
'Land of Hope and Glory' with a fervour I have known
elsewhere only at Conservative Party rallies . . .
plump-living countrymen exercising the privilege of money
to bag a place at an event thousands more would have given
their right arms to see.
(Arthur Hopcraft, *The Football Man*, Harmondsworth:
Penguin, 1971, p. 190)

At the time things looked very different. The 1966 victory
was associated with the Harold Wilson government's desire to
harness the 'white heat of technology'. Ramsey himself personified the spirit of scientific management, rational, ordered
and committed to making technological innovations in the
footballing labour process. He saw the manager's task as the
co-ordination of a team – a collective worker – which would be
more than the sum of its individual parts. He shed the
'backwoodsmen' – the unproductive workers (wingers, in particular) who could not be reshaped into his collective image.
His workers conscientiously subordinated themselves to the
principles of teamwork, and reaped the benefits.

The England team of 1966 was genuinely – in terms of per-
sonnel, tactics and culture – transitional. It was caught in the
movement from the old to the new, losing some of the excesses
of traditionalism (no old-style full-backs here), containing
some elements of change, but by no means wholly or comfortably established in new directions. Ramsey was criticized by
patrician observers of football. In their eyes he had reduced
football to a 'trade', plied by a breed of anonymous journeymen who were to sacrifice spontaneity, flair and creativity.

And the patricians might have had a point. Martin Peters's
'ghosting' play might have been '10 years ahead' of its time,
but Greaves, one of the few proven international stars among
the English players, was left out in favour of the very different
kind of excellence represented by Roger Hunt and Geoff
Hurst. Ramsey's achievement was a remarkable one, to take
on the likes of Pele, Eusebio and Beckenbauer, and to win.
Despite the brilliance of Bobby Charlton and the intuition of
Martin Peters, it is undeniable that the triumph was based
more on caution and determined professionalism than on skill,
virtuosity and flair. Hunt instead of Greaves; Ball instead of
dribbling wingers – the legacy was to leave the English side in a
World Cup wilderness for many years, as the era of flowing
'total football' played by West Germany and Holland left the
English game stranded.

Part of the suspicion with which Ramsey and his team were
greeted by both press and public was generated by uncertainty
about this transition. There was scepticism about the idea of
'tactics' and the team formation (especially when expressed in
numbers such as 4-3-3 and 4-4-2); there was suspicion about
the 'cool' of Bobby Moore, and about the modernist anony-
mity of Martin ('10 years ahead of his time') Peters. There
were few familiar elements amidst this combination; perhaps
Banks the goalkeeper and the Charlton brothers provided
moments of recognition to set against the unnerving prospect
of full-backs who were supposed to 'overlap' and the unlikely
idea of Nobby Stiles and Alan Ball as 'half-back' and 'inside-
forward' respectively (or – as we were to learn to call them –
'midfield players').

In the warm glow of England's victory, scepticism was
replaced by celebration, and from being a team with few stars
the players, preserved in television images, were transformed
into 'personalities': 'Big Jack' Charlton sinking to his knees as
West Germany equalized; the dispute over Hurst's second
goal; Nobby Stiles's 'gap toothed smile' in triumph; and

Moore, hair and composure unruffled, holding up the Cup. Superficially, the team heralded the emergence of a new England, at once more self-assured and victorious. Its essence, however, remained familiar. An imperviousness to wholly radical innovation, vulnerability to foreign competition, a misguided belief in the virtues of Old England – all these elements had their parallels outside football, notably in the looming economic crisis.

All the talk, in sport, politics and economic life was about the need for change. But precious little was done. Changes did take place, but they were all, in that typical 1960s word, to do with style rather than substance. In society as a whole, problems abounded: economic organizations still locked into a nineteenth-century system; political structures which disenfranchised minorities; education systems which privileged a meritocratic elite at the expense of the majority. These remained largely untouched by the white heat of technology promised in Harold Wilson's political rhetoric.

But – as with the trajectory of English football – the symbols of modernization and success now appear more transitory and less profound than their evocation at the time suggested. The Ramsey 'solution' not only failed to overcome some of the structural crisis-problems in the national game, but also had the effect of concealing them from view.

Wilson's modernization was partial and superficial, and was to founder all too soon on the intractability of British capitalism. For all the celebration of affluence, the new classlessness, and social and cultural mobility, familiar features of the British social and economic landscape began to re-emerge. So too with football. Change was in the air – and that was where it stayed. Ramsey's strategy, like that of Harold Wilson, seemed to offer hopes of a genuine recovery of the nation's fortunes. But the short-term success actually militated against the radical structural changes required to make the nation competitive in the post-war world. The organizational problems in the society as a whole were uncannily echoed in football. An antiquated league structure; the failure to compete with other forms of leisure consumption; backward training and coaching techniques. All these proved to be as insoluble as the larger economic and political problems. Victorianism was not buried in the 1960s but merely resurrected in a new, more trendy guise.

England's footballing history has been intertwined in a number of ways with images of British national culture and character. The rhythms of sporting success and failure were held up as a mirror to the changing 'state of the nation', and the personal and collective character of the 1966 World Cup winning team reflected some of the wider social and cultural transitions of Britain in the 1960s. We have suggested that the cultural symbols of '1966' played a central role in the remaking of the 'British tradition' – our society's image of itself. 1966 provides a very sharp reminder of how such traditions are constantly being reworked and revised, while maintaining the sense of unbrokenness and continuity which is essential to 'a tradition'.

1966 marked a transition in English football, identifying the arrival of the 'modern game', and this process of modernization was seen as an adaptation of characteristically English virtues to the demands of world competition. This footballing history provides a metaphor for the condition of Britain. Crisis, decline and uncertainty about our place in the post-war world found dramatic expression in the fortunes of the national team. Similarly, the 'solutions' to decline – both for the nation and the team – offer mirror images. The commitment to rationalizing modernization connects the two – here in the guise of Alf Ramsey, there with the features of Harold Wilson. What is important is how both of these 'modernizations' see themselves as adapting major English/British virtues to the programme of modernization: not slavish imitation of our competitors, but the harnessing of the 'best of British'. In both

spheres, this remaking of tradition served to obscure the
deeper conditions of decline and fostered illusions of a return
to greatness. Each of these images of modernization fed off
and reinforced the other. The fact that this language spoke
simultaneously of modernization and the preservation of tradition is a powerful testimony to the importance of the collective
self-image of the nation. George Orwell once wrote, in wistful
appreciation, of England's capacity 'to change out of recognition and yet remain the same'. It seems an apt comment on the
course of English culture and football's place within it, during
and since the 1960s.

9. NO HOLDING BRAZIL: FOOTBALL, NATIONALISM AND POLITICS

John Humphrey

During the 1982 World Cup final, normal life in Brazil was suspended when the national team took the pitch. For the second-round matches, played at 1.15 p.m. local time, factories remained shut for the whole day, the banks closed their doors at 11 a.m. and huge traffic jams formed around mid-day as millions of Brazilians hurried home to watch their team on television. Families and friends – of both sexes and all ages – gathered around their sets, and the city of São Paulo became quieter than on a Sunday morning. Intermittently, this unnatural afternoon calm was shattered by the burst of thundercrackers released by fans in their gardens and backyards to celebrate the nation's goals.

On four consecutive occasions – against the Soviet Union, Scotland, New Zealand and Argentina – the team's victory was followed by wild celebrations. People flocked to the streets in cars and on foot to mark the victories with dancing, singing and drinking. São Paulo's main avenue, the Avenida Paulista, was given over entirely to music and dance. After defeat in the game against Italy, the Paulista was deserted. The only people to be seen were the street-traders packing up the flags, banners, drink and food that no one had come to buy. The unthinkable had happened. The Brazilian team, with the best mid-field trio in the world, had lost to Italy, a team which had only managed to draw with Poland, Peru and Cameroon.

Football is Brazil's national sport. It was the first professional

team sport to take root in the country, and, in both the
amateur and professional arenas, is still far and away the most
important sport. But this fact alone does not explain the dis-
tinctiveness of the Brazilian obsession with the World Cup. At
club level, the passions aroused by the big teams in Rio de
Janeiro and São Paulo would not appear out of place in Liverpool or Manchester. Active club supporters in Brazil, or
elsewhere, are male and a minority of the population.

When the national squad takes the field in the World Cup,
however, the picture changes completely. The Brazilians
believe that their team and footballing tradition are peculiarly
Brazilian. They regard their country's black and latin roots as
having given risen to a style of football based on individual
flair, agility, artistry (as well as artfulness and trickery) and all-
out attack. As such, football proclaims the value of popular
characteristics and virtues, and it is as deeply rooted in popular
culture as samba and carnival. This was not always the case.
Football had to be captured by the people and fashioned in
their image.

Football first arrived in Brazil in the 1890s, introduced by
the British to an upper-class whose cultural references were
entirely European. The game was played using English tactics
and vocabulary, and its social model was Henley, not
Wembley or Anfield. The game quickly spread to the streets
and wastegrounds, but the upper-class amateurs fought a
strong rearguard action to defend organized football as a game
for the white elite. In the early part of the century, bitter disputes broke out over the use of working-class 'shamateurs' to
bolster the teams of the elite sporting clubs, and the entry of
black players met considerable resistance. It is said that early
in the century, the Fluminense player, Carlos Alberto, caked
his face in rice powder to whiten it before taking the field, and
in the 1920s three players in a Rio de Janeiro side resigned
rather than play alongside a black team-mate. Even after the
eventual professionalization of the sport, black players were at

best only tolerated as employees by many of the clubs which employed them. They were not expected to mix socially with club members.

Even after the game developed a mass following, Brazilian football had to struggle to establish its own style. In the 1930s, for example, coaches imported from Europe tried to impose the W–M formation on Brazilian players who wanted to play in a different style. It was a long time before those in control of football in Brazil accepted that the Brazilian style could compete on equal terms with Europe. In the World Cup too, the Brazilians felt they had to overcome FIFA's tendency to show favouritism to European teams. Brazilians still firmly believe, for example, that they lost the 1954 World Cup quarter-final to Hungary solely because of the perfidious refereeing of Arthur Ellis, of England, whose name became a by-word in Brazil for cheating and treachery.

In this context, Brazil's first victory in the World Cup, in 1958, had an enormous social and national significance. This can be encapsulated in the figure of Mane Garrincha. Garrincha was the great dribbler of the 1958 team. While anyone could admire his football, Brazilians saw in his play the affirmation of Brazilian values over European, and also popular values over those of the elite. For many people in Brazil there was no better sight than a six-foot, blond, superbly-coached and tactically-trained European defender on a rigid calorie-controlled diet being made to look like a fool by the devastating artistry of an undernourished, anarchic black winger with two twisted legs who would never have got past the medical exam in European soccer. In class terms, Garrincha was the semi-literate who could get by on his wits and cunning, able to put one over on the rich and the more powerful (or perhaps the police). His football and his style had a quality which today might be called 'street-wise'. He was one of the boys: clever, artful and cunning.

The 1958 team, then, was the embodiment of a certain

Brazilian way of playing football which finally proved itself
superior to the European style. It had the individual genius of
players like Pele, Garrincha and Didi, combined with a commitment to all-out attack. In the four games which Garrincha
and Pele played together, the team scored 13 goals. In Brazilian eyes, this was a triumph over the European 'strength football', a game based on physical fitness, strong (possibly violent) challenges and subordination to the tactical plan. After
years of social struggle within Brazil for the right to play and to
play as they wanted, and after successive defeats in the World
Cup, 1958 seemed to prove that popular values were superior
to elite values and that Brazil was superior to Europe. It could
not have happened at a better time. The economy was growing
at a faster rate than ever before, the government was committed to a programme of rapid industrial development, and the
working class in the cities was closer to the levers of power than
at any time previously. Brazil was moving ahead both economically and in terms of its football.

With football being so important in Brazil, it is hardly surprising that politicians and government have given it a lot of attention over the years. Football has long been a promotional vehicle for individual politicians, and the organization and voting
structures of the regional federations and the national confederation have lent themselves to patronage and political manipulation. Since there is one structure for all amateur and pro
fessional football, many votes can be won by creaming off
money from the gate receipts of the big clubs and using it to
finance amateur leagues and professional clubs in smaller
towns. The state too has maintained close links with football
since the 1930s, through the National Sports Council, and
there is also a long tradition of exploitation of the national
team for political gain. It is said that one of the reasons for the
Brazilian team's shock defeat against Uruguay in the 1950 final

in Rio de Janeiro was the fact that in the days before the big match, the team's training camp and hotel was invaded by the rich and the powerful. Everyone wanted to be seen with the team. The winning teams in 1958 and 1962 were feted by the governments of the day.

However, the state's conscious use of football for political ends reached new heights in 1970, when the team went to Mexico hoping to win the Jules Rimet outright with a third victory. At that time, the military regime was at its most repressive. The ultra-right within the military had consolidated its grip on power, and the vestiges of civilian and democratic rule had been eliminated. Congress had been closed at the end of 1968, *habeas corpus* had been suspended, and the regime was waging all-out war on its internal opponents. 'Respectable' opponents received the mild treatment of censorship, suspension of political rights and expulsion from jobs in the government, universities and other institutions. Left-wing opponents received worse. The emergence of an urban guerrilla movement was countered by a limited but brutal 'dirty war' of armed clashes, assassination squads and torture chambers directed against all radical opposition to the regime.

At the height of this period of state-sponsored terror, the 1970 World Cup took place. The regime's public relations department made a concerted attempt to increase the popularity of the president and the government by identifying them with football and the national team. President Medici made a point of being seen at important football matches, and of openly declaring his support for two teams with mass popular following – Flamengo in Rio de Janeiro and Gremio in Porto Alegre. The president was free in his opinions about the game, and periodically made recommendations about the players and tactics to be used by the national squad. The propaganda campaign did much to 'humanize' and legitimize a right-wing four-star general foisted upon the nation by a military dictatorship. The special public relations unit attached to the presidency also worked to associate the regime's economic policies with the national football team and its triumph in Mexico. The marching tune, *Pra Frente Brasil* (Forward Brazil), was as much the anthem of the regime as of the 1970 World Cup team, and this was a confusion that the public relations unit sought. They protrayed the triumph of the 1970 team as a victory not merely for the country, but also for the regime, for its policies, and for its vision of a powerful, disciplined and technocratic Brazil. With careful timing, the government chose June 1970 to announce ambitious plans to build the Transamazonian highway, intended to open up the country's vast interior and ease land problems in the coastal regions of the north-east. The government tried to harness footballing euphoria to its plans for national development. The patriotic and pro-government slogan 'There's No Holding Brazil Now' was superimposed on a picture of Pele celebrating a goal.

Football itself was also controlled. Special arrangements were made for the president to see certain games. The players in the national squad were strictly forbidden to make political pronouncements, and the team's manager was suddenly sacked in March, just three months before the Mexico finals. While the immediate cause of his sacking was a much-publicized attempt to confront a rival manager with a gun, many attributed his demise to left-wing views and his refusal to include the president's favourite centre-forward, Dario, in the squad. He is alleged to have said: 'When President Medici formed his cabinet, he did not consult me, and so when I select my team, I have no need to consult him.' Whatever the real motives for João Saldanha's dismissal, it was one more indication that the regime was not prepared to take chances in its manipulation of football.

The blatant use of football for political ends in 1970, and the apparent success the regime had in producing and consolidat-

ing through football a popular presidential image for General
Medici, has led some writers to argue that football acted, and
continues to act, as a kind of super-opiate for the people. The
extreme formulation is that football was used by the regime to
reverse the tide of revolutionary ferment in 1970. More generally, football has been accused of distracting the attention of
the masses from their pressing economic and social concerns
and of de-politicizing popular culture in Brazil.

The more extreme formulation can be rejected out of hand.
The only pre-revolutionary situation in Brazil at that time was
in the minds of the urban guerrillas who bravely risked their
lives trying to spark off a popular uprising which, in retrospect,
was never remotely on the cards. With or without football, the
regime would have survived. The more general criticism of
football – that it de-politicizes and distracts – requires
lengthier considerations, however, not only of 1970, but also
of subsequent World Cups.

Football is never 'outside' of society, pure and untouched by
social and political pressures. In a society where football is so
important, the pressures are even greater. As a cultural
phenomenon, football is the object of class struggle. This
struggle did not end when the game was taken from its elite origins and turned into a mass and national sport. Just as samba
was first repressed and then later domesticated and sponsored
by the state, to be shown off to tourists at Carnival time, so the
state had also attempted to control football and channel the
game's energies in particular directions. In 1970, the military
regime was particularly well placed to use football for its own
ends by channelling popular enthusiasms. Internal opposition
to the regime had been silenced by the closure of congress,
press censorship and the violent offensive against left-wing
opponents. The propaganda campaign around the World Cup
had a clear run.

At the same time, the regime had economic success upon

which to base its appeal. In the three years prior to the 1970 World Cup, Brazil's economy had been growing more rapidly than at any time in its history, and in the major urban centres rising employment, and even rising wages, contributed to better conditions for many. Although the middle-class and the rich took the lion's share of the benefits, growth meant that the urban poor also gained improvement in living standards. The first World Cup to have live television coverage in Brazil was watched by many working people on their own sets. In 1970, government repression was still aimed against the few, while the benefits of growth were more widespread. In these circumstances, football could be linked to a government-inspired ideology of national development and coming greatness, which had credibility because of economic success and the silencing of critical voices.

Even so, it has to be stressed that popular support for the national team and the celebration of its success was by no means merely a creation of the regime. The 1970 team won popular support and admiration because of the kind of football it played. Brazilians do not lend their support to a team just because the government requests it, and they are demanding about standards of play. In fact, the 1970 team left for Mexico without much popular support or credibility. The manager who had guided the team through the qualifying matches had been sacked in March, and the team had not accepted their new manager. The senior players took over team selection and determined tactics. With players of the quality of Gerson, Pele, Tostao, Clodoaldo and Carlos Alberto in the line-up, the result was a feast of football in true Brazilian style. In 6 games, 19 goals were scored, and the team failed to score three or more times on just one occasion, the match against England. The seven goals conceded by the defence were irrelevant, of course. Attacking and winning are what matter to Brazilians, and the 1970 team brought people on to the streets in celebration. The team proved that it was the best, and that the Brazilian way of playing football was the best.

The 1970 World Cup was exceptional, in both political and footballing terms. The combination of sporting success and political legitimation was unrepeatable later in the decade, even though the regime increased its administrative control over football. After João Havelange's departure to FIFA in 1974, the new head of football in Brazil was Heleno Nuñes, a retired admiral and leader of the government party in the state of Rio de Janeiro, while from 1977, the national team's manager was an army captain trained at the military's school of physical education. In spite of this, neither the 1974 team nor that of 1978 were capable of pulling ecstatic crowds on to the streets. By 1974, the regime faced a much greater political oppositon than in 1970. It had relaxed press censorship, and the one legal opposition political party was becoming more vociferous. Popular sentiment had moved against the regime, and football was not a magic ideological weapon which could reverse this trend.

In footballing terms too, the 1974 World Cup team pleased few people. Following the opening 0–0 draw against Yugoslavia, the country's only footballing magazine condemned the team as defensive, disorganized, cowardly and lacking guts. Worse still, the manager had openly proclaimed that he wanted to play in European style, which he summed up as 'do not concede goals, don't let the other team play, only attack when certain'. Brazilian opinion was that the team had been humiliated. It had played the wrong football and played it badly. Perhaps the most damning statistic was a total of six goals in seven matches – half of them scored against Zaire. The soccer magazine's final verdict was that the team had deserved to lose.

Things were just as bad in 1978. Although the team finished in third place, and manager Claudio Coutinho claimed a 'moral victory' because of alleged Peruvian complicity in the 6–0 defeat by Argentina (which put Argentina into the final on

goal average), no one in Brazil cared much for the team.
Coutinho's derogatory remarks on the dribble ('a waste of
time and a proof of our weakness') and his support for European styles and terminology, such as 'overlapping', produced
the reply from one ex-manager that 'overlapping is what Garrincha does by himself'. While Brazilians still hoped their team
would win in 1978, they realized that it did not play like champions and did not deserve to be champions.

Of course, winning does a lot of good for any team's credibility, and Brazilians rarely display much interest in those who
come second. But popular support for the 1982 team, and the
relative absence of recriminations after its defeat, do show a
certain appreciation of pure football. Economically Brazilians
had little to be cheerful about in 1982, and politically they were
patiently waiting for a military regime which had outstayed its
time to devise a formula for transition to civilian rule. There
was none of the economic and political euphoria of 1970. But
the team had, at least, a mid-field of world class (albeit not
comparable to 1958 or 1970), and most importantly it played in
the right style. Based on the brilliant Flamengo team – which,
ironically, was managed by the same Claudio Coutinho who
had taken the 1978 team to 'moral victory' – the 1982 squad
was committed to attack. According to the Flamengo and
Brazil left-back, Junior, the number of goals conceded was
irrelevant as long as the attack scored even more. The team's
poor defence was not, and is not, seen by most Brazilians as a
defect. The team restored Brazilian pride, even in defeat, by
playing in the Brazilian way. The defeat was accepted as an act
of God.

How will Brazilians react to the 1986 World Cup? This is a
complex question involving both sport and politics. Certainly,
popular enthusiasm will only be kindled if the team plays in the
'true' Brazilian style. Footballing values are paramount. But
the direction in which enthusiasm might be channelled and the

idea which people have of the Brazil their team represents will be affected by wider political, social and ideological questions.

From 1950 (the first World Cup brought live into Brazilian homes by radio) through to 1982, the national sentiments underlying support for the team have changed. In 1950, Brazil was uncertain enough of its economic and political future to be profoundly shamed and troubled by defeat. By 1958, rapid industrialization and ambitious development plans had left the nation more confident in its future and more optimistic of solving social problems. In 1970, a similar optimism about development had a much more authoritarian and technocratic flavour. By 1982, confidence had been undermined by economic recession, and football was seen as a temporary relief or a diversion from economic and political problems.

For 1986, predictions are difficult. Had the World Cup been in 1983, the football might have mingled with the mobilization for immediate direct elections for a new civilian president. In the national championship final, the fans chanted the slogan *Diretas Ja!* (Direct Elections Now!) But the regime succeeded in heading off this campaign, and the outcome of the manoeuvrings in the electoral college produced only a half-break with the past. Once again, real improvements in the economic and political situation seemed to have been postponed for the future. New elections for the presidency and the establishment of a constituent assembly to draw up a new constitution might provide fresh impetus, but in the latter part of 1985 there was little popular mobilization or enthusiasm. The government gave the impression of struggling to keep its head above water rather than forging ahead. Such a situation is unlikely to produce national euphoria.

However, there may be no footballing celebrations to be channelled in any direction in 1986. The national team qualified for the Mexico finals quite comfortably, but there is uncertainty about who is to be its manager, and in 1986 there seems little chance of the players saving the team as they did in

1970. At club level, Brazilian football is going through a rough patch. There is no superb team like the Flamengo of 1980–1 on which to base the national squad. Bad club management has crippled the game, as has politicization of the state federations, the national confederation and the national championship. Seasons of ten or eleven months, and the enlargement of the national championship to include smaller clubs in more remote areas of Brazil (a vote-catching device) have taken their toll of players and reduced the sport's attractiveness as a spectacle. Crowds have diminished, and the clubs have come to rely on revenue from television fees. One result of the financial crisis has been the export of players overseas, which further weakens the game's attractiveness to fans and viewers alike. Long-term changes have also had their impact. Urban development has dramatically cut down the amount of free space in which to play football in big cities, and the game has started to take its young players from the schools and sports clubs instead of from the streets and waste grounds. The once ceaseless flood of black talent into professional football is drying up. The 1982 team, for all its merits, showed this clearly. The star trio – Socrates, Zico and Falcao – all came from white, middle-class backgrounds. The likes of Garrincha are no longer to be found, and for the time being the clubs are not well organized enough to compensate for this by adopting a consistent youth policy of the type which led Flamengo to success in the early 1980s.

And yet, who knows? For all its problems, Brazilian football is still a world force. With the right manager, the ageing 1982 team might just win if the general standard is not too high. 120 million Brazilians will be hoping for a miracle.

I wish to thank two Brazilian sports journalists, Silvio Lancellotti of the Folha de São Paulo and Juca Kfouri of Placar, for their kind help and assistance. Information and ideas have also been taken from Janet Lever's *Soccer Madness* Chicago University Press, 1983, Gilda Korff Dieguez (Ed) *Esporte e Poder* Petropolis: Vozes, 1985, and Ruben Oliven, 'The Production and Consumption of Culture in Brazil', *Latin American Perspectives* No. 11i, 1984.

10. A MIDSUMMER NIGHT'S DREAM: ITALY'S 1982 WORLD CUP TRIUMPH

Riccardo Grozio and Mario Flamigni

Translated by Elizabetta Romano

Summer 1970, Mexico, World Cup Semi Final:
Italy 4 West Germany 3

Summer 1982, Spain, World Cup Final:
Italy 3 West Germany 1

In the space of a mere dozen years, the football dreams of a whole nation came to fulfilment. Following the Mexico World Cup in 1978, Italians had great expectations of their national team. The 1982 World Cup triumph fulfilled these expectations, and in so doing broke through a range of traditional divisions – social, ideological and geographic – that mark Italian culture. This happened in a way that led many to interpret the victory as a sign of a national renaissance. Italians of every class and age have been caught up in the explosions of collective joy prompted by the fulfilment of this dream, even people normally indifferent or hostile to the world of sports. But the view that this excitement also expresses a degree of nationalism ignores the realities of Italian history, and most of all the contradictions within that history.

Italy is a relatively new nation, still characterized by a deep sense of locality. Apart from the fascist period, the country has never had a strong and authentic sense of nation. The concept of nationalism, with its emphasis upon the all-embracing and the collective is inappropriate if we are seeking to understand the contradictory complexities of Italian society. A notion of locally-derived patriotism would give a truer picture. To a large extent, Italians see themselves firstly as Romans, Tuscans, or Sicilians, and only secondly as Italians.

Because Italian society is still decentralized, locally-derived patriotism remains an important force. In football terms, this means an exclusive identification with the team of one's own town. Results hardly matter to the local fan, whose support remains total and uncritical. It is different with the national team which is often viewed with a critical hostility. Even the mass media distance themselves from the fortunes of the national team, seeing it not as a coherent entity but as a non-integrated combination of various club teams. Both television and the press amplify disputes and frictions between the various city teams, reflecting the real problems of a country still split by profound divisions.

Since Italy's World Cup victory in 1982, a change in regulations has allowed Italian clubs to sign a second foreign player. As a result, a quite new and different balance of power has emerged within the Italian League. In thirty of the thirty five years from 1946 to 1981 the Championship had been won by a team from either Turin or Milan. This dominance is best typified in the case of Juventus. Winner of no less than five championships in the last nine years, they have enjoyed vast popularity, even outside their home town of Turin. Throughout the country, fans and followers have tended to endow Juventus with 'national' status, an image fuelled by the club's many successes and by a carefully cultivated political profile. This image has been threatened by the dramatic, tragic events of Brussels in May 1985. However, the influence on the club of Italy's most powerful industrial corporation, Fiat and the Agnelli family, has meant that Juventus continues to play a key role in Italian sport.

The other representative of this northern, big-city dominance is Milan – Italy's only truly European city. The internationally famous clubs of AC Milan and Inter have the status of a football academy, and their reputation for excellence has produced high expectations from the fans. To some extent, their dominance has been challenged by the rise of other clubs, most notably Verona and Sampdoria, with the first winning the championship and the second the Italian Cup.

Naples is a different matter altogether. There, the locality's relationship with its team is total and exclusive. Football is lived intensively and emotionally. The arrival of Diego Maradona in Naples for example was marked by a general enthusiasm and a huge rise in ticket sales. Here football is not a concern limited to only a part of the population; rather it is part and parcel of the life of the city.

Roma fans are equally fervent in support for their club, despite the fact that Rome as a city has no great tradition of football success. In 1983, though, Roma's winning of the championship was celebrated with much feasting and festivity in the streets of the capital. The most classic example of this logic of micro-nationalism, however, is Florence. Throughout Tuscany, the presence of both town and team seems to express a historical continuity with the period of the medieval city states. Elsewhere in Italy, supporter involvement with the so-called provincial teams is more unpredictable and tends to depend on whether or not they win. After significant victories a massive enthusiasm develops, while if results are merely mediocre interest wanes.

As already noted, Italy is a culturally divided country. The national team's 1982 victory – following on their much-feted victory over West Germany in 1970 – proved capable of uniting a highly divided society, even if only for one night. National sides returning from World Cup games in Mexico, Argentina and Spain have been welcomed by large popular demonstrations. These demonstrations would not have happened if the sides had not played well. The reverse happened in 1966. Italy's defeat in England at the hands of the North Koreans was a national ignominy which led to early elimina-

tion from the World Cup. As they attempted to slip quietly
back into Italy the team were met with a barrage of tomatoes.
This incident highlights the contradictory relationship between Italian fans and the national team. The relationship is
one of love-hate, marked by constant criticism, even when the
team is performing well, and by total identification when it is
winning. For a decade at least, the term 'Korea' became a
synonym for inglorious or disgraceful defeat – the football
equivalent of Caporetto, the humiliating rout of the Italian
army in World War One. The image that Italians have of themselves is of a self-destructive people, loving all things foreign
and lacking any real national feeling. The Italian people are
rich in history, but it is the image of the emigrant, best of all,
which is indicative of the Italian condition: a rich history but a
poverty of common ideals. This is the source of the famous Italian individualism. The national team has for many years
relied on the creativity and improvisation of individual
players. In 1982, the World Cup was won by the flair and brilliance of Bruno Conti and Paolo Rossi.

Football has become one of the principal secular ideologies
of the contemporary period. It is not that nationalistic currents
do not operate here. They clearly do. Sport offers Italians the
opportunity to throw off the shackles of an ancestral inferiority
complex with regard to other nations. And the victories over
West Germany – at the beginning and the end of this ten-year
world adventure – in one sense represent revenge against a
resented invader. But they are not national victories pure and
simple. Beating West Germany was no simple desire for
national vengeance. Both victories were accompanied by the
waving of blue flags – the team's colours – rather than by Italy's
red, white and green national flag. (Italy's national side are
known as the *azzurri* – literally 'the blues.') This is symptoma-
tic of a general 'azure-effect' that developed after World Cup
victory in Spain. The colour blue developed as a symbol on
other prestigious sporting occasions – for example, *Azzurra*,

the boat that reached the semi-final of the America Cup against all odds in 1983. Some statesman have attributed a strong political meaning to the *azzurro* effect, and possibly they are right.

The World Cup victory in 1982 was the classic 'Italian miracle'. The very unlikeliness and unexpectedness of the victory is the secret to our understanding it. The collective euphoria which it generated has to be understood on this basis: the impossible had come true, in a realization of the dream begun in Italy's prophetic semi-final victory over West Germany in Mexico City in 1970.

Recently the victories and defeats of Juventus and Roma in the European Cup have been greeted by hostile demonstrations from rival fans. When Liverpool beat Roma in the European Cup Final of 1984, the Via Roma in Turin was altered by graffiti to read 'Via Liverpool', – not by Liverpudlians but by Italians from Turin, celebrating Roma's defeat.

Even the dramatic and horrifying events at the Heysel Stadium in Brussels unleashed complex and contradictory currents. After a first wave of nationalist indignation which swept the country and led to some sporadic aggression against British citizens – luckily without serious consequences – the focus turned to the question of who was responsible for the slaughter. Public opinion debated the question: to whom do the dead belong, to Italy or to Juventus? The absurdity of the arguments over the ownership of the dead later gave way, fortunately, to public discussion of the nature of the football system as a whole.

The events of Heysel, and the Italian response to them, are not unique in football. The game is to be seen as the staging of a mortal fight, a potentially tragic contest. Regulations and rules are accepted by players and fans alike: players know the rules of the game; fans abide by conventions of civilized behaviour. Yet sometimes, both on the pitch and on the terraces, these laws are infringed. This is not a new development.

History tells us how many nations have taken measures to ban sports events precisely because they often led to serious disturbances. The excluded, the outcast often have found sport to be an ideal vehicle for the breaking of rules.

Sport, even in the contemporary rational world, remains a mysterious ritual, in which the passage from play to conflict can release contradictory tensions. The Italian dream which came true in Madrid was shattered in Brussels, where the realities of death broke the metaphor of play.

11. OBSERVE THE SONS OF ULSTER: FOOTBALL AND POLITICS IN NORTHERN IRELAND

John Sugden and Alan Bairner

In 1982, Northern Ireland qualified for the World Cup finals in Spain. The team's performance in the championships was a pleasant surprise. The squad was comprised mainly of veterans and fledglings, many from the lower reaches of the English league and a few part-timers from the Irish League. Nevertheless, with a balanced blend of skill, courage, luck and physical presence, Northern Ireland got further in the competition than either England or Scotland. On their way to the quarter-finals, where they were beaten by France, they defeated the host nation 1–0 in Valencia. The achievements in Spain, followed by home and away victories in the European Championships against the powerful West Germans, certainly raised morale in a region dominated by political problems. World championship victories for Denis Taylor in snooker and Barry McGuigan in boxing have been additional morale boosters.

The positive response of most people in Northern Ireland to these sporting developments has been seized upon by certain politicians and the media as evidence of a potential for wider political consensus. Similar optimism has accompanied Northern Ireland's fitful progress towards the 1986 World Cup finals in Mexico (fitful in the sense that it included disaster in Turkey, success in Rumania and the tense 0–0 draw in the game against England at Wembley, which secured qualification).

This optimism, however, is the result of an over-simplified view of the relationship between sport and society. As North-

ern Ireland's footballers were reflecting on the possible consequences of a home defeat by England on the evening of 27
February 1985, a bomb planted by the Irish National Liberation Army (INLA) exploded in an avenue in the shadow of
Windsor Park. This was a reminder that cross-channel sporting encounters were not immune from the Troubles; it was also
a warning from the INLA that participants would henceforth be
regarded as legitimate targets. The return fixture against England was played in London on 13 November, against the
backdrop of an impending Anglo-Irish agreement. This added
a political dimension to the game inasmuch as Unionists,
angered at the idea of Southern involvement in their affairs,
imbued it with symbolic significance. Despite the presence of
Catholics in the team, the game was viewed by Protestants as a
demonstration of Northern Irish determination in the face of
Republican and English perfidy. These political overtones in
the qualifying round are in no way exceptional. The development and character of Northern Irish football in general cannot be understood without reference to its political context.

There are three forms of football played in Ireland: Gaelic,
rugby and association. Of these only the Gaelic game can
claim to be native to Ireland. Both association football (hence
forth referred to simply as football) and rugby football came to
the country in the nineteenth century, through British influence. Football had developed rapidly in the industrial heart-
land of Scotland, a nation with longstanding ties with Ulster. It
is hardly surprising, therefore, that the Irish Football Association (IFA), formed in 1880, was based not in Dublin, but in Belfast, at that time Ireland's most heavily industrialized city.
Centred on Belfast, the Irish League was formed in 1890 and
only gradually did the game expand into other parts of Ireland,
most notably in Leinster, the second most anglophile province
in the country.

A club with strong Irish-Catholic affiliations, Belfast Celtic
emerged in 1891, playing its first games on a rented Gaelic

pitch. Celtic was an imitation of its Glasgow namesake, and its growth quickly dispelled any notion that football was to remain an exclusively anglophile and protestant preserve. For a time, the game was organized nationally and was open to all, regardless of regional, cultural or political affiliations. This harmony, however, was short lived: it ended with Partition.

The setting up of an Irish Free State prompted the Leinster FA to break from the parent body. At once, according to Malcolm Brodie, 'Eire newspaper advertisements described matches in Dublin as being under the "Football League of Ireland" while games in Belfast were merely "Belfast and District".' (M. Brodie, *100 Years of Irish Football*, Belfast 1980) From then on, football was organized separately in Ireland with the League of Ireland and the Football Association of Ireland (FAI) responsible for the sport in the Republic, and the Irish League and the Irish Football Association as the governing bodies north of the border.

Contact between football organizations across the border has not been free from controversy. For instance, at the 1954 Congress of FIFA, the FAI sought approval for its claim that only their representative side was entitled to use the name 'Ireland', a motion, not surprisingly, resisted by their counterparts in the North. However, organizational directives have not always precisely followed political patterns. Ironically, whilst in general the FAI soon resigned itself to selecting players born in the South, the IFA continued to select players on an all-Ireland basis for some considerable time. Questions were raised about this practice during the 1940s and pressure was put on southern-born players to decline IFA invitations. The matter erupted in 1950 when Sean Fallon, a Southerner who played for Glasgow Celtic refused to play for the IFA against the British Army. This affair underlined the complexities of having an association constituted within one political unit making claims on the allegiances of players born in another. The IFA were finally forced to recognize the political reality of a divided

Ireland and the last 'all-Ireland' fixture was played against Wales in Wrexham in 1950. From then on, selection of international sides, like the overall structure of domestic football, followed the lines established by Partition.

Relations between the IFA and the FAI are now more cordial than at any time since 1922. Nevertheless, the structural division remains and the pooling of resources for international competition, although regularly discussed, appears unlikely in the present political context.

Involvement in football has never been exclusive to one or other community in Northern Ireland. However, the nature of that involvement is complicated by existing political affiliations. Participation in the Irish League since its inception has been open to both Protestant and Catholic, but over the years this apparently democratic sentiment has been undermined by broader and more potent sectarian influences. A series of episodes, notably involving the fortunes of Belfast Celtic, illustrate this sometimes divisive character of football.

The early history of Belfast Celtic is littered with instances of crowd disturbance, particularly during games with the city's leading 'unionist' sides, Linfield and Glentoran. Despite the existence of an open recruitment policy, there was no denying the nationalist orientation of the club – the volatile political situation in the Province before the First World War led Celtic officials to consider withdrawing from the Irish League. Further trouble followed in the wake of the 1916 Easter Rising and in the charged atmosphere leading up to Partition. In 1920, shots were fired into the crowd by security forces at a cup replay between Glentoran and Celtic after the latter team's supporters waved banners and sang songs in support of an independent and united Ireland: over eighty people were injured. As Mark Tuohy observes, 'this stupid outburst left a huge stain on Celtic's reputation since they were held responsible.' (M. Tuohy, *Belfast Celtic*, Belfast 1978) The club withdrew from league competition for four seasons, but returned

in 1924 after approaches by influential members of the Irish
football fraternity whose action helped to sustain the League's
apolitical image.

However, the post-Partition situation meant that, in the
long term, Celtic would be the side looked to by those loyal to
the Irish Free State, and would be increasingly perceived by
the Unionist population as a sporting symbol of the enemy
within. The success of Celtic on the field of play and the club's
challenge to the supremacy of predominantly Protestant teams
inevitably engendered unionist resentment. This came to a
head in 1948 when, during the Boxing Day fixture between
Linfield and Celtic at Windsor Park, an accidental clash between Jimmy Jones (Celtic) and Bob Bryson (Linfield)
resulted in Bryson being stretchered off with a broken ankle.
At the end of the game, Linfield supporters invaded the pitch
and in the ensuing violence Jones's leg was broken. As Tuohy
reports, 'a mob stampeded across the Park thirsting for the
blood of Celtic players.' Like all examples of football violence
in Northern Ireland, this incident can only be understood in
the particular context of a divided society; it was the culmina-
tion of long-standing inter-community tensions expressed
through football.

Celtic officials decided that under such circumstances they
could no longer function and, despite a successful tour of the
USA which included a victory over the Scottish international
side, the club folded in 1949. Its disappearance from the
Northern Ireland scene, however, did not mean that Catholics
there abandoned the game. With the exception of Linfield, all
Irish League clubs draw upon the Catholic population for
players, and since Celtic's demise other clubs have served as a
focus for Catholic support. As a result the same political divisions which contributed to Celtic's downfall have from time to
time affected the affairs of other football teams.

This trend has been heightened during the current Troubles.
In 1972, at the height of civil unrest, Distillery Football Club

were obliged to abandon their home ground, Grosvenor Park, because of its sensitive location on the dividing line in west Belfast. In the same year, Derry City were forced to withdraw from the Irish League for security reasons. Derry's misfortunes began with the first riots in the city. The violence which attended the team's matches at the Brandywell on the fringe of the predominantly republican Bogside area, particularly against those from clearly Protestant communities, added to the security forces' difficulties. The matter came to a head in 1971 in events surrounding a fixture with Ballymena United. As Edmund Curran reported in the *Belfast Telegraph*:

> The now customary riot went on nearby to such an extent that there was more noise from the Army's rubber bullets than from the referee's whistle. Ballymena United scored the only goal of the match but lost their coach which was towed off and given a Bogside burning.

Three days after this incident, the club's directors announced that they were moving out of the Brandywell and would play the rest of their home matches in 'neutral' Coleraine. Although Londonderry's no-go areas were theoretically brought to an end by the British army's Operation Motorman, practical considerations by other Irish League clubs and security forces meant that, within the present political environment, there could be no return for senior football to the Brandywell. Crippling debts, incurred while playing home fixtures elsewhere, persuaded the club's officials to suspend operations.

Recently attempts have been made to revive league football in Northern Ireland's second city. However, while the troubles persist, the factors which led to Derry City's collapse in 1972 remain and the Irish League is still opposed to readmission. Moreover, proposals to provide Derry City with facilities for a return to Irish League status have been opposed by local Gaels

committed to the concept of traditional Irish sports. To further
complicate the picture, in the light of local and province-wide
resistance to Derry City's readmittance to the Irish League,
the club has succeeded in gaining entry to the Republic's
League of Ireland. The prospect of a Northern team competing in the League of Ireland has implications not only for the
organization of football, but also for the wider constitutional
arrangements of post-Partition Ireland.

More recently, in the absence of other clubs with obviously
Catholic roots, most of the nationalist football support has
been directed towards the north Belfast team, Cliftonville. In
terms of ownership, administration and players, Cliftonville
would appear to be neither Catholic nor Protestant. However,
because its ground, Solitude, is located close to a predominantly catholic area the club has been appropriated by the locals
as a symbolically Catholic team. So much so that, on the insistence of the Irish League, Cliftonville have had, for the last ten
years, to play their home fixtures against rivals Linfield at the
club's own ground, Windsor Park.

In fact, serious trouble has attended only a few of Cliftonville's games, including one at Seaview against Crusaders,
where loyalist supporters disrupted the match. In the 1978
Irish Cup final, trouble broke out again, Cliftonville fans and
loyalists purporting to support opponents, Portadown. The
police had to intervene in full riot gear. In 1984, during a home
'friendly' against Glasgow Celtic, confrontations between sections of the crowd and the Royal Ulster Constabulary (RUC)
led to violent clashes. On the Sunday before the match, Sean
Downes had been killed by a plastic bullet fired by a member
of the RUC at a Republican rally attended by Martin Galvin,
representative of the American fund-raising organization
NORAID. Only a few days later, the presence of a large contingent of the RUC at a football fixture which inevitably attracted
an almost exclusively Catholic support provoked rage and
retribution on the part of nationalist elements in the crowd.

More recently, Unionist politicians have protested at the behaviour of Cliftonville supporters who, they allege, act as cover for politically motivated Republicans who intimidate Protestant residents by shouting pro-IRA slogans. There have also been complaints about the amount of public money spent on police protection for Cliftonville fans en route to and from fixtures with neighbouring Protestant clubs.

It would be a mistake to draw from all this that the affiliations which surround certain clubs and the crowd problems which beset league football in the Province can be explained simply and exclusively in terms of sectarian division. However, it is impossible to understand even inter-Protestant football rivalry without reference to the wider political context. For example, following a pattern established throughout British football, the most serious crowd trouble at any match held in Northern Ireland in the 1980s took place on 30 April 1983 during and after the cup final between two staunchly Protestant clubs, Glentoran of east Belfast and Linfield from the west of the city. In this particular case religious and territorial dimensions are interwoven, since the 'Blue Men' of Linfield seize every opportunity to stress their sectarian purity as supporters of a club with an exclusively Protestant playing and administrative staff. For their part, the Glentoran supporters, albeit both loyalist and Protestant, are prepared to invert this image and goad their rivals during football confrontations by mimicking Catholic rituals and wearing the green and white of Celtic. This sort of behaviour by loyalists can be understood only in terms of the special relationship between Linfield and Glentoran. The peculiar position of the latter is underlined by the threats of certain Protestant paramilitary organizations angered by this 'Protestant' club's willingness to play Catholics. Thus, even in circumstances which appear to lack a political dimension, the nuances of sectarian allegiances form the backdrop to football hooliganism.

Another dimension is that of identification with football in the Scottish and English leagues. As one might expect there is strong support in Northern Ireland for the Scottish 'Old Firm' of Rangers and Celtic, and this support tends to follow sectarian patterns. When affiliations are directed towards the English League the picture is less predictable. In the past, when clubs like Everton and Liverpool or Manchester United or Manchester City were loosely sectarian, then the support from Ulster was likewise polarized. However, more recently, as the sectarian element in the English League has withered away, so the support of Ulstermen has become more random and diffused. Today it is by no means unusual for political adversaries in Northern Ireland who support rival clubs in the domestic game to share an allegiance to an English club. Thus, the English League can be viewed as neutral territory, and patterns of support for English sides indicate that outside traditional lines of confrontation, Protestant and Catholic in Northern Ireland are able to see beyond the limitations imposed by their divided society.

It could be suggested that at the grass roots football promotes community harmony in Northern Ireland. There are many amateur leagues in the Province and the prospect of thousands of young Catholics and Protestants alike turning out on Saturday afternoons to play the same sport is superficially encouraging. In fact, while it is true that Catholics and Protestants may play in the same teams or in the same leagues, by and large the affiliation of players and community interest tends to break down along lines similar to those outlined for the professional game. Schools, churches, orange lodges, youth movements, old boys' associations, housing estates, commercial and industrial organizations serve to structure league and cup competitions according to locally respected sectarian divisions. Thus, while we can fairly say that amateur football is generally not exclusive, on a closer look it is clearly responsive to the socio-political divisions of the province. Even when Catholics and Protestants play for the same club, this says little except that occasionally, within the relatively neutral context of the game itself, divisions can be temporarily suspended. Once the context is changed, those divisions remain. For example, hunger striker Bobby Sands played amateur football alongside Protestants in Belfast, but as subsequent experience showed, this did not insulate him or his team-mates from taking sides politically.

Things are no less complicated when we turn to the international scene. As the World Cup in Spain demonstrated, many northern Catholics are prepared to support the Northern Ireland international team, which has included many Catholic players. Others, however, see such support as tacit recognition of the Northern Ireland State and acceptance of the Union and turn instead towards the Republic's team. This trend is certainly not discouraged by the fact that Northern Ireland play their home international fixtures at Windsor Park, Belfast, otherwise the preserve of the red, white and blue of Linfield. The situation is even more ambiguous when the two international sides are drawn together in the same competition, as they were in the qualifying rounds for the European Championships. The ensuing crowd trouble between northern and southern supporters during the first leg in Dublin did little for prospects of a revival of all-Ireland football. Similar problems have beset matches between League of Ireland sides and teams attracting predominantly Protestant support, including Glasgow Rangers and the major loyalist sides from Belfast. Protestant supporters seem to view such fixtures as opportunities to assert themselves and travel south to re-enact the Battle of the Boyne.

Nevertheless, there are indications that the groundswell of support for the international team in the North is based upon more than the old post-Partition Unionist ascendancy. The level and depth of the passion characterizing support in recent Northern Ireland fixtures reveals an independent collective identity, which is never so obvious as when cast against the

English. The green and white playing kit which the team wear was once more or less irrelevant to a crowd which traditionally turned out in red, white and blue. Nowadays the colours of the Union Jack are increasingly giving way to green and white scarves, hats and rosettes, albeit with the red hand of Ulster as a centre piece. It is likely that this is a manifestation of a broader shift in the cultural and ultimately political perspectives of the Protestant community, away from the time-honoured union with Britain and towards some form of national autonomy. At this stage it would be dangerous to speculate as to how far this symbolic independence is shared by the Catholic community. What is certain is that when England and Northern Ireland clash at either Wembley or Windsor, it is one of the few occasions when Protestant and Catholic stand shoulder to shoulder united in a desire to beat the Brits, albeit for different reasons. For many Irish nationalists, an English defeat at the hands of any opponent is worthy of celebration – and doubly so if the victorious team is comprised of Irishmen. Certainly, for the Protestants, recent developments between London and Dublin have given additional meaning to longstanding sporting rivalries.

Politicians and sports journalists are quick to point out that sporting activity can help in softening sectarian and constitutional divisions in Ireland, North and South. Sport in itself is neutral, but because it can never be divorced from the politics of its players, administrators and supporters, it necessarily responds to the political currents of the environment within which it exists. In the case of football, despite an occasional capacity to unite across sectarian divisions, the game and its social infrastructure have for the most part served to underline the complexity of inter-community tensions and, in many respects, have played an active part in maintaining an atmosphere in which these tensions flourish.

Thus, as Northern Ireland make the trip to Mexico, no one should be lulled into believing that either the team's perfor-

mance in the competition or the level of cross community support they receive are indicative of a wider feeling for peace and
reconciliation in the Province. The present irony is that the
current success of the Northern Ireland team occurs at a time
when the political situation is extremely volatile and the rival
communities are as polarized as they have been at any other
time during the Troubles. Indeed, in keeping with the time-
honoured battle cry of 'no surrender', Unionist politicians are
pointing to the dogged success of the region's footballers as an
example of Protestant Ulster's determination to resist any
movement towards a united Ireland. Accordingly, when Protestants and Catholics wearing green line up in Mexico and
men from the Shankill and the Falls crowd around television
sets to cheer them on, the outcome of the competition will
mean little in terms of the real issues which keep Northern Ireland divided.

FROM PLAYER TO MANAGER

An interview with Steve Coppell

Steve Coppell studied economics at Liverpool University, during which time he played League football for Tranmere Rovers as a part-time amateur. He spent most of his career playing for Manchester United and won 42 England caps. When forced to retire as a player, through injury, he became manager of Crystal Palace; at 28 he was one of the youngest managers in the history of the game. In his playing days, he also served as chairman of the Professional Footballers' Association (the PFA). He is the author, with Bob Harris, of *Touch and Go* (London: Willow Books/Collins, 1985).

Steve Coppell played in 10 matches in England's World Cup campaign for the 1982 world cup, including 4 out of England's 5 games in the Finals in Spain.

I'd like to ask you to talk about your experience of the game in terms of some of the themes at the centre of Off The Ball. *In your chapter on England in your own book you said some interesting things about players like Maradona, and about what makes the best international managers. Let's start off by talking about your time in Spain in 1982 and about how Ron Greenwood handled the pressures of taking a squad to the World Cup Finals.*

Looking back, I think Ron's preparation must have been quite intense; from the time we got there to the time we left everything was organized. We never thought 'Well what are we going to do now?'. He had so many aces up his sleeve when it came to time, what to do with it, and how to spend it. And that's the biggest killer when you're on tour or at a tournament. Quite often when you're away for 5 or 6 weeks the time tends to drag very very slowly; Ron arranged and prepared things so that you never had those days where you sit down and wish that you could go home – his preparations were first-class.

His handling of the squad came in for a lot of criticism at the end of the tournament because some people felt that he should have played Kevin Keegan; others felt that he should have played Trevor Brooking. He was under a lot of pressure to play them. I think he wanted to play them but Kevin had his injury and Trevor had his groin trouble. So he wouldn't really pick them to start a game. He was quite fair about it. Now whether fairness is a criterion for a good international manager, I honestly don't know.

Do you think he built too much around too few players in the build-up?

No I don't think so. I think the squad of players he had was quite established – there were only two or three places up for grabs, so I don't think it was a case of depending on too few players, or building upon just four or five stars. I think in international football you must get your athletes peaking at the right time. In the year of Argentina – 1978 – we were better equipped than Scotland were. Just before Hungary went to Argentina, just before they departed, they played England at Wembley; we beat them 4–1 and that was a stroll. I often think that it's a matter of peaking, the thing that the Brazilians do so well.

The Italians were pretty good at that, weren't they? Coming from nowhere in 1982?

The Italians, yes, they literally came from nowhere. The first series of games they played – against Cameroon and others – they were average, and yet look at how they came on, ending up by being far and away the best team in the tournament.

Can the manager of an international side control this peaking?

Might England have peaked too soon before 1982, in the good run of the year or two before?

No. The manager obviously has a role to play but other things determine it: the season, the length of the season, the number of games crammed in at the end of the season – all those things make a player stale at the end of a long year. In Italy, they play 30 games. In England we play 42, plus at least 2 Cups, plus internationals, plus, plus, plus. Well, can players play 50 games and then be asked to go to the searing heat of Bilbao and perform at their very best? I think this is unfair to the players.

When you played in 1982 you started with France – later tipped as winners before losing to West Germany on penalties. You beat them comprehensively.

Yes, throughout the tournament we were unbeaten. We won the first round, the first part of the tournament. We'd won our section and things were looking quite good. To be drawn with Spain and Germany was no great problem but I think that after the France game the one thing we didn't have was someone who was really inventive, someone who could create out of nothing, someone – a Trevor Brooking or a Kevin Keegan – capable of lifting us above efficient mediocrity. We were efficient, we were competent, we were competitive, but we were nothing special.

At the absolutely top level must every successful team have one or a couple of those special players?

Yes, against West Germany – and they got to the final – we were opposed by a half-fit Karl Heinz Rumminigge, with Stielike at the back. Those two players made the difference.

Why do you think the England side so often doesn't seem to have that special player? You can think of Alan Hudson, Peter Osgood, Tony Currie or Glenn Hoddle, the sort of player that seems to have this creative midfield ability. Why have they never established themselves in an England squad?

I wouldn't see any of them as having the quality or calibre of the kind of player we're talking about – with the exception of

Glenn, who's still yet to prove himself, but is well capable of doing it. In training, he's the most gifted player I've seen, he really is.

Why don't we produce as many of this calibre of player, with that extra something, as other countries do?

It's probably got an awful lot to do with the Grand National that is the Football League, 42 games in different and difficult ground conditions. There isn't really the room for that individual talent. If you're playing in a team – well, I would much prefer to have 11 fellows who would run their guts out for 42 games, rather than one player who won't play all the time plus 10 others, one player who would be absolutely magnificent for 2 games, very good for 8, average for 12 and crap for 20. I would much prefer to have consistency and I think most managers think like me.

I've only seen Platini on television. You've seen him and played against him. What do you think he's like? Do you think he's the type of player who has brilliance and consistency too?

Oh without doubt, without doubt. He is exceptional. I think he's consistently good. When he has a bad game he's still OK.

So in Britain, we've got too crowded a programme for generating real excellence at international level?

Yes. Look at the Liverpool sides. They're so good, yet there's nobody like that in their sides. Except possibly Dalglish, but even he's never really made it at world level. Liverpool remain a team, first and foremost a team, and then they're individuals within that team.

Do you think there's anything in the 1982 Finals in Spain, after the opening rounds, that Ron Greenwood could have done to bring out more from the squad? You went home undefeated, but without quite making it . . .

No. I hope I'm not sitting too much on the fence here, but I honestly can't think of anything, even with hindsight. Perhaps a gamble with Kevin Keegan and Trevor Brooking – that would have been a helluva gamble though, a helluva gamble to

take. England needed to beat Spain by two clear goals to pip
the Germans on goal difference. They drew with Spain in a
goal-less match. After 63 minutes of that match, Ron Greenwood pulled off Rix for Brooking and Woodcock for Keegan.
Brooking and Keegan then missed the two clearest chances of
the match, and England went home undefeated, a whisker
away from the semi-finals. Not surprisingly, as the two substitutes were able to make such an impact in such a short time,
Greenwood came in for a lot of criticism.

What do you think of Bobby Robson's prospects for Mexico?
Well, he's got everything going against him. This time last year
I would have said he had an excellent squad. Since then they
seem to have lapsed down again. I think there's the climate
against them, and a European team has never won in South
America. He's got an awful lot going against him. It's going to
be the end of a very crowded season, with players playing often
twice a week through the season, a tremendous burden for any
international player.

You commented in your book that you were pretty happy about
Scotland's failure in 1978.
Well, yes I was absolutely delighted at that after what Mac-
Leod had said about me. [In the England-Scotland match at
Hampden Park in 1978, Coppell scored England's winner,
picking up a loose ball after a cross from Peter Barnes. Mac-
Leod was quoted in the papers afterwards as saying that the
second worst player on the pitch crossed for the worst player to
score the only goal.]

Why do you think that Ally MacLeod built things up and acted
as he did? Do you think it was the media's fault?
I think he was receptive to being built up. He was happy to
hear people say that he was what he thought he was. He just
got carried away and couldn't control himself, and it ended up
with people looking his way for trouble.

It's not coincidental, then, that the players themselves were out
of hand?

No – in terms of discipline, the man at the helm is the one who's responsible. And that's the manager.

Which manager impressed you in 1982?

It was very much a mature managers' tournament. Durvall with West Germany, he'd already been team manager for a long time. And there was Hidalgo with the French, and Bearzot in charge of Italy. I distinguish between the good club and the good international manager. The latter has got that ability to cut himself off from a very intense situation and sort of sit back and watch the flowers grow. He needs to lean back and relax and let the players relax, especially when they are competing at the top level. They can only do it if they have periods of relaxation. You get the young feller who's tearing at the job – well it might work for a week or two, for a fortnight or so, but after that, you're going to get some problems. [Robson himself started off his England career, in Coppell's view, as a newcomer 'tearing at the job'. After Greenwood, there was an 'immediate and startling . . . change in atmosphere and attitude', involving more intense sessions, even on Sundays, and 'somewhat spartan conditions at our new training centre,' as Coppell puts it in *Touch and Go* (p. 139)].

So you think that Ron Greenwood got it right in 1982 and Bobby Robson might get it right for 1986. Would Don Revie have been able to do what you think's needed if he'd hung on?

Well, Don Revie proved that he couldn't. He was a club manager. I think he himself would admit that now. He was a club manager and not an international one; he couldn't stand not having day-to-day control over his players.

In Spain, did you see much of the other players from other sides?

No. We played our games, and in between the games we had hotels to ourselves. In Bilbao we had a hotel to ourself which was very quiet. We were isolated for just about all of the time.

So you didn't see much of other teams. What about the fans: were they in any way hostile?

No. Even throughout the Spain game – I was injured and wasn't playing, I was in the crowd – the crowd was responsive and appreciative of good football. At the France game there was some hostility, but it was directed at the English supporters, who were provoked, rather than at the English team. Just before the French game it was said that if there was trouble it would be the fault of the English fans. I've seen, with Manchester United when we've been playing in Europe, provocation of United supporters that was unbelievable. We played in Valencia once. The team bus arrived and as soon as the team bus arrived, the United supporters like any good supporters, got round the bus and started chanting. They were no harm to anybody at all. Then 5 or 6 policemen on horses came along with batons and started beating them. It's unbelievable that there wasn't a reaction.

The fans didn't react at all?

They didn't react. They just took it. United fans were being beaten around the head and shoulders by Spanish police and they didn't react. Whether they'd react now I don't know, things have changed.

But you can't recall any examples of fans on the rampage in the 1982 World Cup?

I was vaguely aware in the French game of seeing some disturbance in the crowd, but I'm not sure what it was.

How aware are you when you're playing of problems on the terraces? I recall some of the Liverpool players after the Brussels tragedy saying that they'd had no idea what was actually going on. They were either in the dressing room, in the tunnel or on the pitch and playing.

When you're on the pitch . . . yes, there have been occasions when there have been problems and I haven't noticed them. But I think you usually sense the atmosphere of the crowd and the ground. I'm usually quite aware of them.

Who do you think were the outstanding players of the 1982 finals?

Platini, and the Brazilians. . . . In lots of ways the Brazilians were the best team. They were wanting to show everyone what a good team they were, instead of just being professional. The great players were Socrates, Zico, Falcao. I liked some of the German players too, like Breitner. But I don't think Maradona really gave of himself in the tournament. He didn't perform. He was only 22 at the time and every time you turned on the television you'd find him there, advertising coca-cola or something else. The burden placed on him was obviously too much to handle.

You say in your book that he 'sold his soul to Spain'.

If he'd had the mentality of a Bobby Charlton, or a Bjorn Borg, I think he would have concentrated more fully. In this World Cup he's got more of a chance to show us just what he can do.

Might he have left Argentina too early in his career?

No. It was possibly a good time to leave Argentina, when he was known as the best player there. He had to broaden out onto the world stage sooner or later, so off he went to Barcelona. It didn't really work for him there, but he's now playing well in Italy for Napoli, a so-so team. He's the most gifted player in the world, and it shows even without a good team.

Did you ever consider playing on the Continent?

Yes at one stage when I was coming to the end of a contract. But I'm a typical Cancer. I often thought that if you go to Germany or Spain and you go through a bad spell, it must be the loneliest feeling in the world, not knowing a lot of people, not being more than partly fluent in the language, not being accepted even in your trade. So I'm not saying that I wouldn't have gone, but Manchester United made a good offer to me to stay.

Do international matches and tournaments act as a cattle-market for players?

Yes. There are an awful lot of agents at them. Agents do all the deals. International agents are licensed by FIFA, and they do all the deals. Many deals are struck with players from the winning teams.

Some people have an image of you all in your hotel in Bilbao, being sneaked up to with whispered offers from some undercover individual.

I don't think it's quite as cloak-and-dagger as that, but I'm sure it goes on, especially with the African countries, probably the one big untapped market.

What's your view now, as a club manager in England, of the movements of players between countries? Especially with things like large-scale unemployment for youth in our own country. Should there be an international movement of players?

The PFA and the Home Office have probably got the right balance at the moment; the only people who are allowed to come into this country are established internationals, people who are far from cheap labour. If it were an open market we'd have, for example, lots of 16- or 17- or 18-year-old Scandinavians coming in, and we'd lose our direction. I think the balance is right on that one.

In your view, did the way Ramsey got the 1966 England team to play have a big influence on the development of the game?

Yes, it was the way they played, the way they did things. It's like the long-ball theory now. If England went to Mexico and won using that strategy then we'd see everyone using it, whereas at the moment they're most sceptical of it. Alf Ramsey was successful with his own version of 4–4–2 and no wingers, and everybody followed him.

As a winger yourself, do you think people were right to follow him? Having tried Connelly and Paine, Ramsey then abandoned the winger.

Well, he got results. Geoff Hurst scored consistently throughout the tournament. And there were Bobby Charlton and Bobby Moore. If you look right down the centre of that team – and it's down the centre where you're going to score from anyway – then what was his strongest side? Jack Charlton, Bobby

Moore, the fullbacks, Bobby Charlton and Geoff Hurst – the jigsaw fitted nicely at the time.

But if you adopted a Ramsey scheme with less good players wouldn't that lead to a sterile pattern of play?

Yes. But without good players, you'll get beaten, whatever strategy you use. I might have a vision of how I want my own team to play, but because of the players I've got there's no way I can approach that. We play our way, and that might be totally different from what's in my mind's eye. I've got Mickey Droy at the back, he's 34. I can't get him to change his way of playing. And Jim Cannon, a good player, excellent. I'm not going to change the way they play now, and I wouldn't really want to. They do their jobs efficiently.

There is the view that despite all of Ramsey's achievements, despite the great 1966 success, he's had a pretty bad influence on the game in the mid- to long-term. Some people claim that since Ramsey the game has got less exciting.

I don't agree with that. He did the best he possibly could with the players he had. To be a good winger too you've got to be really outstanding on the day.

This view argues that the 1966 victory might have been the point at which flair started to die in the British game. We won the World Cup, Geoff Hurst was the first player ever to score a hat-trick in a final, but he wasn't, some think, ever as good as the dropped Greaves.

Well, in the end, nobody will really remember the Brazilians from the World Cup in 1982. The teams that are remembered are the winners. And there's also the fact that here in England we've never had enough outstanding players. We have good players, but the special ones – Garrincha, for instance – those with exceptional spark, we've not had them. On the whole you just can't argue with Alf Ramsey: his track record was second to none, even though he didn't make it to the 1974 Finals.

What can you remember of the side Ramsey took to the 1970 World Cup Finals in Mexico?

Most of all, I remember Brazil as probably the best team I've seen. Always going forward, with confident and very special players. They defeated England 1–0 in an exceptional match. The Brazilians were a magnificent team, and the two teams' respect for each other was clear to see. That England team, too, was great.

And then they lost to West Germany in the quarter-finals.

Well, that was one occasion when you could criticize Alf Ramsey on his substitution decisions when he had the game sewn up. [England were 2–0 up with only 22 minutes left in this game at Leon. The German manager Schoen had revitalized his side with a fresh attacker, the winger Grabowski. Germany pulled a soft goal (under Bonetti's dive) back and then Ramsey substituted Colin Ball for Bobby Charlton and then, Norman Hunter for Martin Peters. Germany equalized, going on to win in extra time. Back in England the TV pundit Malcolm Allison ripped off his Union Jack tie, throwing it onto the ITV studio floor.]

In the World Cup how can the manager sustain the squad's morale when you're all so cooped up and locked in?

It's very much the spirit of the 22 players. It's a very strange number really, 22, when you think about it – you've got 5 subs. Now if those people sitting up in the stands aren't feeling a part of things, aren't happy, you've got problems. No matter how happy a manager is and how happy the trainer is, if the players in the group aren't happy you've got no chance. The atmosphere comes from within and we were lucky in as much as we had people in our 22 who didn't play, players who didn't get changed, but kept themselves involved.

Did you keep up with the other matches in the Finals, watching television for instance?

Yes. We had days off from training. One day we went to a sports club, played golf and tennis, you were always active and wanted to be active.

How were relations with the Press?

We met the Press at the end of training sessions. You had a chance to do an interview at, say, midday for an hour. You soon get to know the journalists you can trust. With the others, if they ask a good question you give them an answer, but they don't always write your answer. I suppose nobody enjoys to see crap written about them, but we're professional about it and we learn to ignore it.

Do players see the World Cup Finals as a lucrative money-boosting event?

Some do, certainly, but I think everything's sorted out now with the players' pool.

Do you think the Press is unfair or cruel in its treatment of individual figures?

I think it's got to be cruel. The World Cup is the pinnacle, it's where people are judged forever and a day. Jimmy Greaves is remembered for not playing there.

You've played in Europe for United, at Wembley for United. Was the World Cup the really big and most memorable experience?

It is the tops. You can't go any higher. You've got the best players in the world there. In the FA Cup you've got some of the best players in the country, in the European Cup you've got the best in Europe, but in the World Cup it's the best players in the world.

Does it feel so good even if the stadium's not full?

Oh, yes. It's great whatever the crowds. For the first game I felt more nervous than usual. But after the first game it's like anything, once you know you can do something you might get nervous but it's good nerves rather than destructive nerves.

The nerves are a way of building up to the event, not worrying about it. Yet some players can just freeze.

That's what happened to Peter Bonetti in 1970. He just didn't perform on the day.

What's next for you? Raich Carter once said that every former professional footballer should be shot at 35; that's a bit extreme!

You've been in the World Cup, in Europe, in big matches with the most famous of our English club sides. How do you feel you'll cope with getting older?

Well, it's hard, that one. Carter may have been referring to cynical ex-pros. I hate to see a feller who's had a very good living from the game saying how much it's changed and 'it's not as good as when I was a player', or 'people aren't as good, players aren't as good'. When I was playing, I resented seeing all these people coming on television and slagging off the game and I made a vow that I'd never become a cynical ex-pro, always going on about the greatness of his days and his game.

Some of them are just sad that they're no longer at the centre of things, they can't find a place equivalent to that. Tell me, what would you have done in Bobby Robson's shoes?

Well, if I'd have been Bobby Robson preparing for this World Cup, I'd have loved to have got my players together for one weekend every month from the New Year in – January, February, March, April, May. One weekend for each of those 5 months so that you could get your players to train together, get some kind of spirit, just something to get some unity within that group. And I would love the season to be finished by the end of April so that there's more preparation time. Not as much as other nations perhaps, as I think the English mentality couldn't cope with too much preparing for just the one tournament. But at the end of April, to finish the season and have a fit, healthy squad, moving into scientific acclimatization work.

Why have we never done this?

Well, it's the structure of the Football League. There are 92 Football League chairmen all having different opinions, and all with the bank manager knocking on the door, and pay-as-you-earn knocking on the door. With all those creditors, they can't see the season finishing in April with four months without money coming in.

An old English disease – parochialism?

Yes. It's not wrong that the League should generally take preference over the international team, but in World Cup year, the England team should take precedence.

How would you finish a season by the end of April?

I'd just cram games in, get the season over with.

And would you make it a condition that players in the squad, on national duty, would have to be there regardless of their club's position in relegation or promotion battles?

Yes, very much so. I don't think it will ever happen but you never know.

Would it appeal to you to be manager of England?

In about 25 years' time I would probably say yes. It's only when you're a lot more mature and you know you can handle the job that you should take that on. Billy Bingham once said that you shouldn't be a manager under 40, because it's only when you get past that age that you can have some kind of appreciation of the job in relation to life. There are times when I agree with him.

Steve Coppell was interviewed by Alan Tomlinson.

Biographical Notes

Alan Bairner and John Sugden lecture at the University of Ulster at Jordanstown. They have both written extensively on sports, politics and leisure. Their article is based on their essay 'Northern Ireland: Sports in a Divided Society' in the collection *Sports and Politics* edited by Lincoln Allison.

John Clarke is a lecturer in social policy at the Open University and is co-author of *The Devil Makes Work* published by Macmillan, 1985.

Stuart Cosgrove is from Perth, Scotland. He has written extensively on soul music for *Black Echoes, City Limits* and *New Musical Express* and co-authored the book *Theatres of the Left*, published by Routledge & Kegan Paul in 1985. He is a visiting lecturer at the West London Institute and Media Editor of the *New Musical Express*.

Chas Critcher lectures in communication studies at Sheffield City Polytechnic where he also teaches on the Sports Studies degree. He has previously published articles on leisure and on football. Other collaborations with John Clarke include *Policing the Crisis* (Macmillan, 1978), *Working Class Culture* (Hutchinson, 1979) and *The Devil Makes Work* (Macmillan, 1985). A lifelong suffering supporter of Brentford FC, he still occasionally referees and plays football, despite advancing age and an innate lack of ability.

Mario Flamigni is a researcher in leisure studies. He specializes in the relation between sport, performance and theatre.

Christine Geraghty works for NALGO and teaches a Film Studies evening class for the British Film Institute. She has written about *Coronation Street* and other television serials, and is a loyal follower of QPR.

Riccardo Grozio is a sports journalist specializing in the relationship between sport and culture. He lives in Genoa, Italy.

John Humphrey teaches sociology and Latin American Studies at the University of Liverpool. He wrote *Capitalist Control and Workers' Struggle in the Brazilian Car Industry* (Princeton University Press 1982), has researched on Brazilian society for 12 years and is currently completing a book on the sexual division of labour in Brazilian industry.

Tony Mason teaches at the University of Warwick. His publications include *Association Football and English Society 1863-1915* (Harvester Press, 1980) and he is presently working on a book entitled *The British Soldier in Two World Wars*.

Steve Redhead lectures at Manchester Polytechnic. He has written extensively on law, crime and deviance, and sport and leisure. His book on British professional football in the 1980s, *Sing When You're Winning*, is published by Pluto Press, 1986. His current research interests are in the field of popular culture, especially British pop music in the 1980s.

Philip Simpson has worked in various colleges and polytechnics and is now head of the Education Department at the British Film Institute.

Alan Tomlinson teaches at the Chelsea School, Faculty of Social and Cultural Studies, Brighton Polytechnic, where he teaches courses on sport, leisure and popular culture. He has edited collections on sport and leisure, and is currently editor of the international journal *Leisure Studies*. With Garry Whannel, he co-edited *Five Ring Circus: Money Power and Politics at The Olympic Games* (Pluto Press, 1984).

Stephen Wagg is the author of *The Football World* (Harvester Press, 1984), and teaches sociology at East Warwickshire College in Rugby.

Garry Whannel teaches the Open University Popular Culture course. He is the author of *Blowing the Whistle: The Politics of Sport* (Pluto Press 1983), co-editor with Alan Tomlinson of *Five Ring Circus: Money Power and Politics at The Olympic Games* (Pluto Press 1984), and has written extensively on the television coverage of sport.

John Williams from Bootle in Merseyside is a Liverpool supporter. He works in the Sociology Department of Leicester University, and with Eric Dunning and Patrick Murphy is co-author of *Hooligans Abroad* (Routledge & Kegan Paul, 1984).

OTHER BOOKS FROM PLUTO

FIVE RING CIRCUS
Money, Power and Politics at the Olympic Games
ALAN TOMLINSON and GARRY WHANNEL

'If this system were given to a third-rate world power, it would make them a second-rate world power.' A Motorola representative commenting on the communications network his company is supplying for the LA games.

On 28 July, the 1984 summer Olympics began in Los Angeles, the dream-factory of the world. But what about the venerated Olympic ideal of amateur athletes competing for the love of sport? Did this ideal ever exist in the slave society of ancient Greece?

Five Ring Circus takes a historical look at the myth and reality of the Olympic movement. It contains chapters on nationalism; apartheid; women; the media; business; and the Olympic cold war. '

128 pages
0 86104 769 9   £2.95 paperback

BLOWING THE WHISTLE
GARRY WHANNEL

Sport is part of society, not an apolitical world of
its own. Its organization, finance, and even the
dominant values of sport are rooted in politics.
It is a popular activity that is controlled by the
ruling classes and dominated by men.

Blowing the Whistle outlines previous
socialist attacks on sport. It argues for the
possibility of more progressive forms of sport
and sport organization, rooted in social
ownership and democratic control.

128 pages
0 86104 508 4   £2.50 paperback

ON TELEVISION
STUART HOOD

Stuart Hood looks at the way the words and
images used by television cameras are chosen,
who chooses them, what the organizations are
in which the broadcasters work, and how these
organizations are linked to the central power of
the state.

'The best little book about the medium to be
published for some time.' *Time Out*
'Needs to read by anyone who thinks
television is worth caring about.' *New Society*
'An adept and rounded critique.' Anthony
Smith, Director of the BFI

144 pages
0 86104 702 8   £2.95 paperback
Rights: World, Pluto Press

Pluto books are available through your local bookshop. In case of difficulty contact Pluto to find out local stockists or to obtain catalogues/leaflets (telephone 01-482 1973).